Voices From Faringdon

Faringdon Writers

Volume 8

VOICES FROM FARINGDON – Vol.8

Disclaimer

Published in 2023 by Kindle Direct Publishing (part of the Amazon group of companies).

Copyright ©2023

All rights reserved. No part of this publication may be reproduced, stored in any retrieval system, or transmitted in any form or by any means, electronic, mechanical, photocopying, recording or otherwise without the prior written permission of the copyright holder for which application should be addressed in the first instance to the publishers. No liability shall be attached to the author, the copyright holder or the publishers for loss or damage of any nature suffered as a result of reliance on the reproduction of any of the contents of this publication or any errors or omissions in its contents.

Designed by Faringdon Writers

Printed in the UK by KDP

ISBN: 9798375288413
Imprint: Independently published

Compiled and edited by Val Hughes

Cover image provided by Scharlie Meeuws

Foreword

Thank you for choosing to buy our 2023 anthology! This is the eighth annual volume of work from Faringdon Writers.

Inside you will find work written to an agreed list of selected themes including an ekphrastic poem (one stimulated by a piece of art) and accompanying non-fiction piece, a short dialogue, eulogies - fictional and for a favourite writer, and a few crime stories.

Faringdon Writers continues to flourish with an ever-increasing number of members. This edition features pieces written by twelve current members, including voices old and new.

The aim of this book is to showcase their many talents and is intended to give a purpose to, and an outlet for, their creative skills. The following pages are therefore filled with a wide range of offerings. Some will make you laugh, others provoke an interest, and we hope will always provide the impetus to sit, relax and read. I am sure you will agree that the results are somewhat amazing and dramatically different in both content and style.

So please read on and enjoy…

VOICES FROM FARINGDON – Vol.8

Contributors

David Burridge   p.7

Sue Cain p.13

Hilary Coombes p.25

Sullatober Dalton p.43

Barry Eames p.69

Val Hughes p.87

Scharlie Meeuws p.117

Diana Moore p.121

Sam Tindale p.125

Elliot Van der Hyde p.143

Peter Webster p.157

Jocelyn Wishart   p.187

VOICES FROM FARINGDON – Vol.8

DAVID BURRIDGE

David Burridge has been a published poet for many years, appearing in magazines such as Acumen, Orbis and Dream Catcher. He has also published four poetry collections (Pausing for breath along my way, Making Sense, Child's Play and Streetwise). His fourth collection, Streetwise, is published by Cinnamon Press. Describing himself as a "gentle pragmatist", he now has time to indulge his love of philosophy, having retired from a career in business and employment law. David is a fluent German speaker, a keen walker, and a passionate European. He lives in Oxfordshire with his wife.

I Know What I Like!
(Or do I? An aesthetic experience in the Tate Modern)

I go into the House of Art to feel its visual power. My eyes
are stormed from every side, by shape and line and colour.
Landscape scene in primary red - I expected green.
Pure mechanism in an artist's head - a non-utility machine.

Sculpted shapes twist and turn in my line of vision.
Assembled with precision, a mixed-up map of Britain
Did the artist vent the need to head north to go south?
Or was she on an aesthetic - *just stay put* – mission?

Box of random articles suddenly takes on meaning.
high piling rubbish becomes an exhibition.
Is everything a work of art? Or am I really dreaming?

The guide assures me every artefact is an arty-fiction
True to life is just a lie. A portrait with four heads is a
delicacy of perception. I'm troubled with one of mine.

Has the world no natural order? Just Random objects in our
minds

Waiting for us, at our leisure, just to suit our personal pleasure.

Is order then a concocted rhyme?

I look to leave this puzzle-world of colour line and shape.
But where does the exhibition end; is there no escape?

The Tate Modern is an art gallery located in London. It houses the UK's national collection of modern and contemporary artwork. It is located in the former Bankside Power Station, in the Bankside area of the London borough of Southwark. Its deployment could be viewed as a massive piece of contemporary artwork.
Years ago when I worked in London it was a routine of mine to wander in to its predecessor-The Tate Gallery, which had a wide mixture of art from the past and present. It was a random and free step of discovery. My first encounter with Tate modern was a bit of a shock as I have explained in this poem.

Satan's Sulk
(A bronze by Fouchere 1807-1852: showing Satan seated with his wings wrapped around him)

His toned torso hunched in a bronze-wrap of wings.

A demon mask of disgust as he smells humans working out – no chance of heart failures just yet.

He is fit to run a marathon – could catch any stray,

but can't keep pace with performance enhancers.

Claws manicured to scratch a scream, lightly drum impatience,

as if waiting in a nail-bar queue, only to be told:

torturers tear out nails for nothing.

Searing eyes now dull as smoke - evil is at hand but he is booted out.

Who needs to be pushed off the straight and narrow in this urban bang?

Hanging around crossroads is pointless if they all get lethal jabs.

Gone are the good old epochs when a decent Dr Faustus could be

Persuaded. Or a Don Giovanni making a bassful final scream.

And as for that gig in the wilderness – win some lose some!

It is the personal service that is missing today.

Humans have terror on stream - it's turning digital – holocaust without a password needed.

Worse still ---------

Oh Hell I am just a metaphor!

Satan's Sulk, Property of The Clark Art Institute, Williamstown, Massachusetts, USA

SUE CAIN

Sue has lived in Faringdon for over 20 years with her family. She is an avid reader and likes to write as a hobby. Faringdon Writers Group has given her a reason to hide away for a few hours and get writing. Travelling through France, Spain and Portugal over the last few years has given inspiration for some of her work.

Starry Night by Vincent van Gogh

Starry Night by Vincent van Gogh currently owned by MOMA in New York

Starry Night was painted in 1889 by Dutch painter, Vincent Van Gogh, shortly before his death 1890.

This painting belongs to a small series of 'nocturnes' initiated in Arles with 'Café Terrace at Night' and followed by 'Starry Night (over the Rhone)'.

Van Gogh painted Starry Night in Saint-Remy-de-Provence during his stay in the Saint Paul de Mausole Institution. He admitted himself to the asylum after infamously cutting off his ear to silence his hallucinations the year before.

Depicting a semi accurate view from his window just before dawn, where the moon and stars cast their light. A shadowy cypress tree stands in the foreground, blocking part of the view, the hills beyond loom above the village and church. Only tiny flecks of light penetrate, yet further away, the moonlight and starlight dominate the night sky.

This seems to be a painting of two halves; in the lower half reside solid objects, the village and church, and the fields and hills. The upper half is a sky full of movement, nothing is still.

Van Gogh's technique of impasto, brush strokes of thickly laid-on paint on canvas is well known. In this painting the more solid objects have brushstrokes which flow downward whereas the brushstrokes of the celestial objects flow predominantly side to side. Van Gogh uses the lines and swirls to create movement in the heavens and shimmering light from the stars.

The painting currently resides in the Museum of Modern Art (MoMA) in New York City and is worth more than US$1 million, approximately £800,000.

Starry Night

Day is spent, the sun no more
Descent of darkness to the core.

Swirling stars on midnight blue
Flicker and shimmer with silver hue.

Golden moon gives celestial glow
Amongst the stars few clouds can flow.

Dark shadows fall from cypress tree
Over the village towards the sea.

Elusively hidden in myopic haze
Streets and paths beyond one's gaze.

The tall church spire reflects the light
In the distance hope shines bright.

The world holds its breath as it waits for the day
When demons are banished, voices held at bay.

More Than Just a Housewife – Edith Bramble 1918-2021

We are here today to remember Edith, much loved mother of Florence and Ethel and grandmother to Lucy, Charlotte and Victoria. Born in Acton, west London, in 1918, she lived through two world wars, saw monarchs and prime ministers come and go. Lengths of skirts were shortened shockingly, and technology progressed beyond her wildest imaginations.

Many of you here will only have known Edith in her later years when she sat knitting jumpers for the grandchildren and making her famous apple pie. 'No-one can make apple pie like grandma' declared Victoria at the age of four, her mother recalls. But she was so much more than just a housewife.

Edith was brought up by her mother and aunts along with her own beloved grandmother. These women were supporters of the Suffragette movement and were quite probably early proponents of women's lib.

Edith felt her childhood to have been of no consequence. She went to a good girl's school in West London, close to where she lived. She learnt French and German, was good at maths and enjoyed drama. Growing up as an only child, Edith was indulged and as a result was an unusually large child. Despite this she was part of the lacrosse team. She had a few close friends, recounting to Victoria at one point that they used to get up to all sorts of mischief but tantalisingly didn't go into any details. During her final years at school she became a boarder and would frequently climb out of the window to meet someone her mother would have considered unsuitable. In fact, one such meeting led to her finishing the year early and spending some time away with distant family at the seaside in Clacton.

Although too young to remember much about the first war, she was greatly affected by the lack of male role models and seeing little need for a man in her life she chose to keep the child and become a single mother. Not once but twice. Neither of the girl's fathers played any role in their lives. Ethel notes that she and Florence just accepted the status quo. However, the advent of WW2 meant Edith could remain respectable by styling herself as a widow. Although Edith did not really care for such notions, she felt it would be best for the girls.

With childcare support from her mother, Edith was able to join the WRENs at the outbreak of war. Originally assigned to work in Eastcote, Edith was able to visit the girls regularly. There was then a period that Ethel recalls when mummy didn't come home for years. Edith only spoke about this in later life, but at the time no-one knew where she was, whether alive or dead.

Some research into family history by granddaughter Victoria, brought to light Edith's role in SOE, (Special Operations). She was posted to Northern France where she remained for two years, organising resistance, aiding in sabotage and gathering information that would aid the allies prior to the D-day landings.

Returning home after the war was tricky for Edith, she missed the excitement and adrenalin rush of her resistance days and was always looking for something to fill the void. A few years after the war, determined not to become just another 1950's housewife, Edith began work for the BBC as a world-renowned war correspondent. Over the following twenty years she covered many of the major of conflicts, giving her the adrenalin rush she needed, but also leading to the breakdown in relationships with her daughters.

However, recollections from the family, show that there were some occasions that stand out as attempts on Edith's part to repair the damage, including being bundled into a mini for a family holiday to Skegness. Edith was no diminutive figure, and the squish factor was considerable. 'Lucky, we hadn't got the dog that year! Said Charlotte. Granny, me and Lucy in the back with Violet sprawled across us. Our knees up to our elbows because the footwells were full of Granny's tipples. Not that we knew what that meant. Mummy had the front to herself because she needed space for the map.

But size never stopped her. Edith was a keen hill walker. Each weekend, when back in the UK, she would choose a destination reached by train and head to the hills. Walking all day, she would then pull out a packed lunch and flask to enjoy. This was a passion she tried to instil into her daughters. Florence recounts that many a weekend they would be kitted out in waterproofs and forced to march up hill and down dale. Unfortunately, this only reinforced Ethel's hatred of the outdoors and Florence's determination to move to warmer climes. Florence is joining us by Zoom today from the south of Spain. Sadly, not even her mother's death can tempt her back to the damp of West London.

Edith always took her role as grandmother very seriously. Despite much badgering from the grandchildren she never gave them rubbish to eat. No lollies or ice creams unless it was a special occasion. Ahead of her time, Edith had become a vegetarian shortly after WW11. The treats, Lucy recalls, consisted of courgette surprise, courgette scones, courgette cake and best of all courgette ice cream. It was a good year for courgettes but a bad year for sweet treats.

She was always one to keep up with the times, being an early adopter of the mobile phone. 'Those that looked like a brick.' she would tell people, 'Don't you remember?' She quickly mastered each new generation and loved today's technology and the smart TV. Up until her final couple of years she would video call the family at the most awkward moment. She had a liking for the Baltic crime series' and enjoyed nothing more than a good murder.

The care home staff noted that she enjoyed a sherry every evening and no matter how poor her eyesight became she could still pour the required amount with a steady hand into her favourite glass. It wasn't just sherry she had a penchant for. Port, brandy, and red wine were all favoured and could be drunk in copious quantities. In fact, her favourite evenings would be those spent drinking all the other residents under the table. No-one knew quite how she managed it.

We will each miss Edith in our own way. I hope that recalling some of the highlights of her life will allow you to understand the abrasive and sometimes cantankerous lady of her later years and discover someone ahead of her time whose life story would not be out of place had she been born 100 years later.

HILARY COOMBES

Hilary Coombes is a bestselling author of women's contemporary fiction, including 'The Hen Party' that topped Waterstones fiction list when it was published. She has also written non-fiction books for university and college students.

She was born in Devon and worked in many occupations from librarian to ice-cream seller at the roof top café of a department store. She studied education and special educational needs at university and worked as a teacher in further and higher education, specialising in teaching visually impaired students ... a job she loved.

Once her children left home, she abandoned real life drama for the secrets of fictional families. Her latest novel 'SIBLINGS. Kit's Story' will be published in 2023.

She now lives with her husband between Stanford in the Vale and Spain although their number increases to three in Spain because a local Spanish cat always adopts them when they're there.

Find out more about Hilary on https://hilarycoombes.com

The Visitor

The house was in the middle of the terrace. I rang the bell, keeping it pressed for a little too long. The door inched open and hesitantly a thin woman peered around the half-open door. 'Yes? What d'you want?'

'I need to talk to you.'

'Oh you do, do you.' She started to close the door and I pushed my foot between it and the frame.

'Gemma, it's about Tom, your ex.'

Now I had her attention. She looked me up and down and then stood to one side to let me pass.

My eyes scanned the room. It was surprisingly clean and tidy with a huge television in the corner. I made my way to the sofa and sat.

'Well?' She glared at me expectantly. 'How do you know Tom and how did you find this address?'

'From Tom's phone.' I said, not taking my eyes from her face. 'I presume you're Sarah's Mother.'

Her eyes widened. 'How the hell d'you know that?'

'That's unimportant. It's your daughter who's important right now.'

A silence settled over the room during which Gemma sat opposite.

'Do you know where Sarah is?' I asked.

'She's with Tom at his flat.'

'You sure?'

'Course I am.'

'When did you last see her?'

'What's that to you. You a policewoman?'

'No, I'm a friend. So when did you last see Sarah?'

Her face revealed her dilemma. 'Well, probably last month.'

'Probably?'

She shrugged. 'It might've been longer.'

'Sarah told me she hasn't seen you for six months.'

'Jeez, that's a l ...' I caught her eye and the word 'lie' seemed to stick in her throat.

'I'm not judging you. I'm simply asking.'

'Okay, maybe longer. But it was Sarah who walked out on me. She said she wanted to be with her dad.'

'Why do you think that was?'

'Humph. What teenager wouldn't want the freedom Tom gives. He doesn't make her go to school, gives her money, let's her smoke and God knows what else.'

'Don't you think a fifteen-year-old needs some guidance. Needs her mother?'

'I got fed up with the battles to be honest. My life's quieter now.' She nodded. 'It's better.'

'Better for you maybe, but what about Sarah?'

'She doesn't need me.'

'Oh, but she does. She told me so.'

'You! Told you?'

'Yes. Last night when Tom brought her to my flat.'

Gemma stared at me open-mouthed.

'Tom brought Sarah for me to train.'

'Train? Just who are you?'

'I'm a prostitute. It's good money, but it's not a life I recommend. Not one your daughter deserves.'

'You'll find Sarah here.' I push a piece of paper into Gemma's hand and make for the door. She doesn't speak, but I can tell she's moved.

As I walk away from that depressing house, I feel sure that tomorrow Sarah will be home. Home with her mother.

And Tom? He'll get exactly what he deserves, and my orchard of retribution will gain another apple.

The Mark of Death

Renting a shoebox sized flat in the City of Bristol is expensive even on the outskirts. Unfortunately my flat is shoebox size and one that could only ever fit a child's shoe inside. My workmate, Megan, also rents a shoebox so over coffee at work one morning we hatched the idea of pooling our resources and moving in together.

We found a fantastic flat online. It's nearer the centre of the city than our existing flats and boasts three bedrooms, so naturally we jumped at it. Once we'd moved in, we realised that three bedrooms was an exaggeration. The box room is just big enough for a small bed and not much more, plus its small window faces a brick wall. We use it as a storeroom. It's handy for all those useless bits and pieces that everybody accumulates thinking they might come in handy one day. They never do though. We never learn.

At first all went well. Megan and I are both tidy people and like the same music and food, so we got along like a house on fire. However, we soon realised that even two salaries left very little surplus once we'd paid the rent and bills. So we had no alternative but to advertise for a third person and hoped that someone would be desperate enough to want our unappealing box room.

We put an advert in the local shop window and the first person to reply was Emily. I hadn't expected Megan to be so keen when we interviewed her; she even offered her a lift to work each morning because she said she passed Emily's office. This was an outright lie.

Megan and Emily's friendship flourished, and I must admit I felt left out. For the first month I managed to bite my tongue at the way Megan fawned over our new flatmate, but things were about to change when Megan's relationship with her married lover came to an end. I believe the breakup was for the best, a relationship with someone married can only end in tears. However, there was no way I could persuade Megan of this, and she wallowed in self-pity and depression.

It was about this time Emily asked if she could invite a friend to stay and we stupidly agreed. I say stupidly because when Jack arrived complete with suitcase it was a bit of a shock. He looked like a student in need of a wash and he smelt of that skunky, musky, odour associated with marijuana (I had to Google the smell to find this out).

He wasted no time in telling us that in his view education was a total waste of time, and it soon became obvious that he put paid work in the same category. He quickly got his feet under the table and in no time he was sharing Emily's bed full-time and living scot-free off everyone. The nightly sounds coming from Emily's bedroom drove Megan insane and had I not known better I would have judged her as being jealous.

'He's smoking pot, eating our food and we're the mugs making life easy for him. He's got to go.' She screamed at the top of her voice one Sunday afternoon when it was just the two of us at home. I was afraid she was about to burst a blood vessel as her whole face turned crimson and a vein popped out in her neck.

It was clearly evident that Jack had no intention of moving out and as he was aided and abetted by Emily who'd paid six months' rent in advance, we found ourselves in a difficult situation. It was at this stage something flipped in Megan. She changed from a fairly easy going individual, albeit still depressed at times, to someone who was given to sudden bouts of nervousness and at times seemed poised for flight.

I was worried.

Megan's declining health forced her to apply for sick leave from work. She said the doctor mumbled something about acute depression and anxiety and issued bucket loads of antidepressants, which I'm afraid to say turned her into a zombie.

It was now Emily's turn to change, and Megan became the centre of her attention, she waited on her hand and foot. Nothing was too much trouble. Whether it was genuine feelings of compassion towards Megan or whether she was tiring of Jack I'd no idea, but the day I came home from work early and found Emily and Megan lying naked on the lounge carpet, hands exploring each other's body was a shock. A primeval rage surged through my body. How dare they flaunt their sexuality making me feel angry and uncomfortable. It was only much later I admitted to myself that I'd felt a little envious of their happiness.

Whether Jack was aware of their relationship at this point I don't know. But I do know his reliance on drugs increased fourfold when Emily left him to sleep alone and moved in with Megan at night.

This is when I dearly wished I'd enough money to rent my own flat because the arguments between Emily, Jack and sometimes Megan were unbearable. There were times when putting my hands over my ears was of no use.

One particularly volatile Saturday night I watched the three of them, hatred in their eyes, voices shrill with anger, and a nameless dread engulfed me. That was the night Megan slapped Emily across the face and Jack punched Megan in return. The uproar that followed must have been heard next door and all my efforts to calm things down failed. I escaped to the nearby pub.

When I returned a few hours later I was greeted by a spaced-out Megan asleep on the lounge sofa. Her breath was jarring noisily from her open mouth which dribbled brownish saliva down her slack jaw onto the white cushion beneath her head. I decided that the cushion had no chance of ever being white again. There was no sign of anyone else, so I made my way to my bedroom hoping the night remained peaceful.

I was first up on Sunday morning and the quietness was uncanny. Megan was still asleep on the sofa although she was breathing quietly now. When she opened her eyes a little later, she really wasn't with it. I asked her if she'd like black coffee and she nodded. However by the time I'd returned with the mug she was asleep again. I left her slumbering and made my way to the kitchen for breakfast. Then I read the news on my phone, put dirty clothes in the washing machine and vacuumed the lounge, all the time expecting someone to emerge from one of the bedrooms. Nobody did but at least Megan was now sitting up on the sofa. She looked dishevelled, her pale face and the dark circles under her eyes didn't exactly give her a morning glow. She gave me a strange smile, her eyes brimming with tears. Then she opened her mouth, but no sound emerged. It was like a silent lament.

Jack appeared next, his dirty clothes and lack of interest in grooming was nothing unusual, but his eyes were more bloodshot than normal, and his defensiveness scared me. He stared through me before shouting aggressively that I should stop glaring at him. I wasn't. I turned away and walked to the kitchen.

It seems I was the only person hungry enough to eat lunch even though it was only a cheese sandwich, and it was an hour or so later I raised the idea that perhaps we should wake Emily. Megan shrugged and Jack ignored me, although he probably didn't even hear as he was slumped in the chair, head thrown back, eyes closed and mouth wide open.

Another hour passed before I raised the subject of Emily once more. 'My goodness she must be tired, hope she's okay. I reckon you all had a great time when I was out last night.' My words fell on deaf ears.

Half-an-hour later I made a cup of coffee for everyone and as I brought the tray into the lounge nodded towards Emily's room. 'Do you think Emily would like a drink?' I asked as I lay the mugs on the coffee table.

'Maybe.' Megan said distractedly. 'It might help her hangover; I expect she's got one, I certainly have. We were all high last night.'

'I suppose she's alright in there?' I asked looking directly at Jack who simply shrugged and turned away.

Megan now looked concerned. 'Do you think we ought to check?'

'She's probably fine, just zonked out after a heavy night.' I smiled weakly at Megan. 'Tell you what I'll make her some black coffee.'

Megan knocked gently on Emily's door as I balanced a strong coffee and a bottle of water on a small tray.

'Try knocking a bit louder.' I ventured.

But it was of no use, no matter how loud Megan hammered there was no response from within. 'Do you think we should go in?'

I nodded. 'She's probably simply sound asleep.'

However the sight that met us as the door opened caused Megan to scream loudly. "Oh God. No,' she yelled over and over.

Emily was slumped on the bed, face upward. Her motionless right arm, hand splayed open, was dropped over the side of the bed and from what I could see there was one big bruise the entire length of her arm. Her legs were outstretched, feet crossed.

Her head appeared to be resting on the pillow, but as we approached, we saw that her eyes were wide open and staring at the ceiling. It was her skin that made me shiver for it had taken on an ashen, bluish colour, something Megan obviously noticed as well for her terrified eyes sought mine. She pointed to Emily's neck where we could clearly see a horizontal ligature mark. The dark, dried blood had soaked into the bedclothes giving a vile metallic scent that smothered my senses making me gag.

Megan howled as she backed away from the bed, her eyes locked onto the lifeless body before us. It was then the tears fell, hers and mine mingled together as we held each other in a tight embrace.

Time blurred and I moved as if in a trance. I remember phoning the police; I remember Megan screaming and screaming as she shook Jack angrily; memories of the police cordoning off the bedroom and talking to us individually in the kitchen is something etched in my brain which I long to forget.

When we all came together later that evening, we compared the questions we'd been asked by the police and the answers given. I didn't admit that I'd told the police of a row I'd overheard when Jack threatened to kill Emily, neither did I think it wise to let them know I'd revealed how frightened Emily was of Jack. I felt that was something for the police to consider and decide whether it was relevant. People often say things they don't really mean don't they.

We all felt that the police were keen to establish whether Emily had many visitors and whether we thought she might have let someone unbeknown to us into the flat that night. None of us believed she had and as I was at the pub most of the evening I was of very little help.

It was a couple of days later that the police returned to the flat with a warrant to search. Jack ranted loudly and stormed around the flat like a hurricane out of control. At one stage I was afraid he was about to punch one of the policemen, luckily Megan calmed him down before this could happen.

When they cautioned Jack and asked him to accompany them to the station Megan and I were shell-shocked. My legs wouldn't stop shaking and astonishment grabbed me by the throat and strangled any coherent words. At first, I didn't dare look at Megan's face and for now the grip of her hand and the silence we shared was sufficient. The things to be said could come later, right then words were unwilling to take flight.

We learned later that the autopsy findings were consistent with death due to ligature strangulation and no other major injuries were noted. Emily's time of death was estimated to be late evening, a time which placed Jack and Megan in the flat.

I'm not surprised that eventually the Crown Prosecution Service charged Jack with murder. A smack head, out of his mind, with a temper and a foul mouth that I knew he would use at the police station. That of course plus Jack hadn't made a very good job of removing Emily's blood from the belt hidden under his bed.

It was over a year later that I am called as a witness for the Crown. As I stand in the witness box I can't stop shaking and my eyes are drawn to Jack, I can't help it. My blouse sticks to my back but it isn't the heat. It's panic. I don't want to be here, and I don't want to hear any more. It's forcing me to revisit memories I'd prefer remained buried.

Observing myself from my mind's eye I'm pissed off at my own reaction. Fuck's sake woman, why are you worried? Surely everyone's already decided that Jack's guilty, he's not going to be coming home ... a drug addict, a waster who hadn't even smartened his appearance for Court and when he started shouting and ranting at the Jury surely he sealed his own fate.

He was given a life sentence with a stated minimum term of twenty years.

It was a relief when it was over and behind my eyes the tears started. I wept on and off for two full days. Now all I had to do was get on with my life.

All this happened a long time ago. I'm proud to tell you that Megan and I are now married. Yes, Megan is my wife and we're very happy together. It was always meant to be, and her infatuation with Emily was simply a hiccup on the way to realising that it was I who was meant to be her soul mate.

The night I stole home from the pub and murdered Emily was the best thing I ever did. Of course being at the pub gave me a bulletproof alibi and luckily nobody saw me leave or return from the rear entrance near the ladies toilet. A perfect place to remove my plastic clothing protection and wash my face and hands afterwards. I was missing for less than ten minutes, hardly time to powder my nose.

I promise you I'm not normally a violent person, but that night I was angry. Angry with the way both Emily and Jack treated my love. Megan deserved better than that.

Strangely the killing had been easier than I imagined. When I slipped home from the pub, I'd been met by the sight of an inebriated Megan asleep on the sofa and I prayed that Jack and Emily had gone alone to their separate bedrooms.

I carefully opened Emily's door and there was her solitary body asleep on the bed. I soon realised there was no need for me to creep around her room for she was stoned out of her mind, whether on drugs or alcohol I'd no idea, maybe it was both. A lightweight like her was no match for an angry woman, and boy was I angry. There's something addictive about anger rather like self-harm so not in a good way. Not that I self-harm, at least not anymore.

The idea to use Jack's belt only occurred to me when I realised that all three of them were stoned out of their minds. Luck was definitely on my side, and I smiled to myself as I threw the bloodied belt under Jack's bed.

I will carry these experiences with me for the rest of my life. I'll never get the images out of my head, but that's okay. I'll keep growing and living now I have Megan in my life.

Megan and I are going on holiday next week. We've had quite a few holidays together since we married, this time we're heading for the Bahamas. Sometimes I wish I could tell her everything, everything I've been hiding from her all these years. But of course I don't. I've no idea what her reaction might be, and I don't want to spoil the good thing we've got going. Anyway what if she threatened to go to the police? That would never do for I've no wish to be forced into murdering the person I love best in the whole world. I've come to the realisation that there's no changing the past and I've got a future to deal with. So that's just what I'm doing.

I would like to thank Gavin Hernandez for giving so generously of his time advising me on the legalities of police and court procedures. His input has been invaluable. Thank you, Gavin.

SULLATOBER DALTON

When asked about his background, Sullatober said the first known mention of Dalton in the British Isles is of a French Archbishop arriving in Ireland. It seems the archbishop had married one of the French king's daughters without his permission and had to flee that country. A fine romantic heritage for a writer, but then I'm from a family of a story tellers and it may not be true.

The Dancers

**Dance Me to the End of Love by Jack Vettriano
copyright Jack Vettriano Publishing Limited
Company www.jackvettriano.com**

This Jack Vettriano picture, showing a young man and woman, seen from behind, ready to start waltzing at a ball, attracted me as it reminded me of my first date with Elice. It shows the couple as the sole occupants of a dance floor, grey and white like calm water on a sunless day.

The man is in black, presumably a dinner suit, the woman in a white gown, bare shouldered but wearing long white gloves.

Both are dark haired, as we were, hers piled up in a coiffure.

The picture is black, white and grey, misty and dreamlike. A muted halo surrounds their heads, drawing attention to the flesh colour of the woman's bare shoulders and the man's cheeks at the 'ideal horizon' in the top half of the picture.

The couple obviously know each other but are uncertain about the future; her hand sits lightly on his shoulder; his arm is not tight at her waist, but round her with natural ease; they are touching at the hip but not close like lovers; their heads are drawn back, alive and expectant in their attitude.

The woman is on the right. Beyond her, half her size in the middle distance, is a female figure, her partner hidden, waltzing flamboyantly, presumably how the woman imagines the dance of life will continue.

To the left of the man, much further away and more dreamlike, is a male figure, back to the viewer, shielding his female partner and showing how he feels they will dance into the future.

It could have been us.

A Quickstep into Life

We stand with footsteps ready and expectant
For life's long dancing game to start.
Her fingers resting lightly on my shoulder,
Her smile laid just as softly on my heart.

But will living have a waltz's classic grace,
The quick and urgent footsteps of a foxtrot,
Will the sexy sliding of a Tango have its place?
I wouldn't like the cloying sweetness of a violin quartet
I'd prefer my footsteps guided by a mellow saxophone,
And answering to the wailing of a Ragtime clarinet,
Or swaying to the sighing of a silky slide trombone.

But what of her?
Is there a chance, she'll join the dance?
For I must be a rover and not a stay at home
Must go to make a living where I've never been before.
In the far-off land of Hiawatha
Or where the ocean laps the darkest Afric shore.

Well, she's sometimes soft and gentle
Then at times a dancing queen
Sometimes treats living with abandon,
Sometimes most proper and serene

But wherever we are meant to travel
In this or in some far off, foreign land
Her smile says we will go together,
When the music starts, we'll take each other's hand.

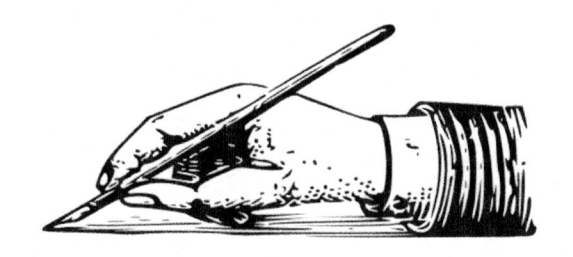

Jinks

I'm surprised to see so many at this memorial service, as most of you must have suffered through Hugh Wallace. I see several looking confused, so I'll use the name we knew him by, Jinks.

Jinks came into the world like any other child, but the similarity didn't last long. Miss Kirkhope will remember the school being closed when he discovered stink bombs. While Cortez may have stared with a wild surmise at the Pacific, his excitement was a shadow of the excitement Jinks felt when he found the mayhem such smelly inventions could create.

Despite all the chances life had of avoiding it, Jinks grew to adulthood, or near enough for him to convince the recruiting sergeant he had reached that state, and served in the war as a sniper. I'm sure you will all know that he spared one German's life because the soldier had gone to relieve himself. Jinks waited for him to finish, but an officer appeared and began hustling the man back to his post. Jinks decided to teach the officer a lesson. He always maintained that the soldier waved his gratitude.

After beating Hitler, Jinks went to work in the mines around Cairndhu. The coal mined during the summer was stockpiled on the surface behind a retaining wall of large lumps. In those days, all heating and cooking, even boiling of clothes, was by a coal fire. There were some old people who could not always afford that luxury, and a miner neighbour would take one of the lumps to the pensioner. This upset the mine manager and, during one summer, he had the winter stockpile whitewashed to prevent stealing.

A few mornings later, it was discovered that a section of the wall was no longer white. Some lumps had obviously been stolen, and an investigation was started to find the culprit.

Jinks had been on night-shift and came to the surface to find the place in turmoil.

Jinks looked at the wall, smiled, and turned the 'stolen' lumps back to their original whitewashed side. There were some who blamed Jinks for the trick. Nothing was ever proved, but the whitewashing was abandoned, to the relief of several pensioners.

Jinks was a regular domino player, but rarely in the traditional sense. Several saw him play both ends to finish a game, but were so busy laughing at his audacity that the incident, instead of being punished with disqualification, passed into local legend. There are other stories in the same vein, but they might embarrass those still living, and I will not repeat them here.

To the astonishment and confusion of several of the community, Jinks later became one of the local postmen, giving him access to postcards and telegrams, and he became, in some ways, the local historian. At times, Jinks used his reading of various communications to create confusion and anger among those whom he felt were too snooty - Jinks' expression, not mine - or needed cheering up with what he considered a joke, a joke which was not always appreciated.

In later life, something Jinks never acknowledged, he took Alice Wailey under his protection, leading her into several adventures that brought excitement into what had been a quiet and humdrum existence, as she herself admitted. One of her favourite adventures being the time Jinks saved her from a raging bull by throwing his bicycle over the animal's horns. The Royal Mail wanted to charge him for the damage to the bicycle, but Jinks had enough goodwill in the community to escape any punishment for such a heroic act.

No one seems to have informed the Royal Mail Jinks had been using the bicycle for joyriding, with Miss Wailey on the parcel shelf, and not for its intended purpose of delivering parcels.

We can all remember Jinks delivering Christmas mail in his Father Christmas costume, a ploy that brought him and the local postmaster annual reprimands from those in higher positions, reprimands that were overlooked the following year until someone complained.

Jinks never married, whether this was to avoid his mischief being curtailed, or from fear of a serious commitment, is not known.

Although devil-may-care, there was a serious side to Hugh Wallace when the community was threatened and when the Flower Show looked like being taken over by Cedeco in 1954. Jinks put his shoulder to the wheel and acted as secret agent, keeping those directly involved in the show's local management informed of Cedeco's plans.

Some people are heroes because of their courage and integrity. Jinks would have laughed at the idea of himself in that role, but he never did anything mean to those who were vulnerable, or took advantage of the weak. In fact, rather the reverse, often making the recipient of his jinks realise they had been mean, or thoughtless, towards others.

While there may be some who are not disappointed at Jinks' death, Cairndhu has lost something of its character with the passing of his cheery smile, his never quite perfect, yet never untidy uniform, and his pranks.

Sir Walter Scott – a Eulogy

Walter Scott was born into the closes of old Edinburgh where sanitation was primitive and disease rife. The city's nickname, Old Reekie, comes from the smokey coal fires and the smell of sewage that pervaded its narrow streets and alleyways. Guardeloo, was often heard in Scotland's capital, warning that bed pans and similar receptacles were about to be emptied into the walkways. Walter contracted childhood polio and walked with a limp and a stick for the rest of his life.

At two, he was sent out of the smog to live with his grandparents in the border country, where his grandmother entertained him with stories of the raids and conflicts in the border region in earlier times.

At four, he returned to Edinburgh to the house in the New Town the family had moved to and began to grow tall. His increased height brought worries his frail body would be unable to carry his weight and he was again sent to the borders, where he met James Ballantyne, who later became his publisher and business partner.

At twenty-one, Walter, qualified as a lawyer, became more and more involved in writing, translating from the German for Ballantyne. He collected the ballads of the border, and began to write what were known as historical romances, much of it in rhyme. The Lady of the Lake and Marmion, based on the Scottish defeat at Flodden, being the best known.

He was asked to be Poet Laureate in 1813 but turned the honour down and it passed to Robert Southey.

Scott turned to writing novels when Ballantyne's publishing house, of which he had become a silent partner, ran into difficulties. Wary of being considered too frivolous for an advocate, his work was published under a pseudonym. The success of his writing made anonymity a subject of universal controversy and he was forced to admit authorship. Originally serialised, Scott's stories generally start slowly with a good deal of deposition, but once started, the plots are well devised, and several - Ivanhoe, for example - have been turned into successful films. Edinburgh's Waverly Station getting its name from another.

Becoming Sir Walter in 1820, Scott was the ideal man to arrange King George IV's visit to Scotland in 1822 and took the opportunity to make a display of Highland dress, including the ceremonial tartans of the clan heads. Through this, the kilt has become the only proper dress for all Scots, even the Lowlanders, for whom, instead of being romantic, a claymore wielding, bare arsed, kilted Highlander would have been something to fear and avoid.

When the printing firm declared bankruptcy, Scott, at the age of fifty-four, refused to follow suit, put his home and assets into the hands of his creditors and wrote until he was able to reclaim everything; a mammoth task.

He did not have long to enjoy his final triumph, dying of a heart attack in 1832 at sixty-three.

Two's Company

'Alec! I didn't know if I'd recognise you.'

'I'm older, wrinkled and short of hair but still Alec. You still look aristocratic, Grace.'

'Thank you. This is my son, Frank. He'll be back for me in half an hour. Off you go, Frank.'

'Tea?'

'Coffee, Alec.'

'It was good of your son to bring you.'

'Good! He's frightened this might be some kind of grooming thing.'

'You never know, I might want to sell you a gold mine in Africa.'

'Spain! I could be gulled into going to check it out. Be held hostage and turned into a slave. Why did you call? It must be thirty years.'

'Marge told me your husband had died and gave me your number. When I was working, if someplace came into my mind unexpectedly, I didn't hesitate, just went to investigate. So, when I dreamt about you.'

'He died five years ago. So, what did you want to talk to me about? Young Frank thought you might want to get me to withdraw my savings and run off with you.'

'There was a time . . .'

'I thought there was going to be. But you just vanished.'

'I had to go to India . . .'

'It was supposed to be for three months!'

'It lasted longer than I expected. When I came back you were . . . I went round to your house a couple of times, but you were out with someone else.'

'Your mother could never tell me when you were coming back, so, when Edgar asked me to go out, I went.'

'Were you happy?'

'Were you?'

'Lena coped, but was never comfortable at company functions.'

'Marge said your wife was good looking.'

'She could look stunning; the centre of attention, which she hated, and made things worse.'

'I was never stunning, but I think I kept my end up.'

'Vivacious is the word I'd use. People always wanted to talk to you. Like that chap near the window.'

'He's called Badger. One of those touchy-feely people who make you feel unclean. Ignore him. I wouldn't have done that yesterday. You're a bad influence, Alec.'

'I am? We've been together less than an hour and I'm ready for a ploy.'

'So, if you haven't been up to any ploys, what have you been doing?'

'I wanted to organise events, but Lena talked me out of it. So, I've spent five years in a room making model boats. Suddenly, it feels like waiting to die.'

'Ready, Mother?'

'Thank you for coming, Grace. I'll be here next Wednesday. Think over what I said about that gold mine in Spain and..."

'What's this, Mother? You haven't signed anything?'

'As I say, Grace, I'll be here next Wednesday.'

'Mother won't be coming. I have a meeting and can't bring her.'

'I have till next Wednesday to think it over. Karen can bring me.'

'We'll talk about this in the car. Isn't that Mr Badger over there?'

'Yes, and if you speak to him, I'll box your ears. Now, let us make a dignified departure.'

The Writing's on the Wall

I'd stripped the wallpaper from half of the first wall of the room when I found the first piece of the map. All it said was Buchan W. I was mildly curious but didn't think much of it. Then I got another piece on the second wall. The pieces were kind of stuck back to front behind the wallpaper and came off clean.

I had just started on the third wall and what I had stripped off was lying all in a heap, when Gwen, who owned the bungalow, came in with tea.

'It's a nice bungalow,' I said, took a drink of tea, and was about to tell her about the papers, when she started talking.

'Yes, I was lucky to get one in this complex. My daughter Sandra found it for me after the man who had it went to jail.'

'To jail?'

'He robbed a bank or something. He put that hideous wallpaper on, it's too busy for the room and…'

I wasn't really listening. If a bank robber had taken the trouble to hide a sketch map behind the wallpaper, well, guess what the map was for? To show where he had hidden the loot of course!

'… he had this fixation with John Buchan, the chap who wrote the "Thirty-Nine Steps"…'

So, that was what Buchan meant! Thirty-nine steps W – West!

I don't know what Gwen was saying at the time, but I interrupted. 'Do you know how much that bank robber chap stole?'

'Two million or something.'

Two million! And the clues were behind the wallpaper! The writing really was on the wall!

I took the rest of the paper off as quickly as one of those silent films, then scrambled among it, until I had all four pieces of the map.

They were stuffed inside my overall when a youngish chap, about thirty, five years older than me, came in. He looked me over and, while I'm middle height, slim and feel attractive - I'd like to say svelte but I think you have to be Swedish for that - I don't have the kind of bosom you can hide things in and I was worried the papers I'd stuffed in there would be obvious, but he just smiled and went to talk to Gwen. I carried on clearing up. I heard him trying to talk Gwen into selling but didn't pay too much attention, beyond hearing his name was Geoff.

The map was easy to follow. Well, the sun sinks in the west, doesn't it?

'Finishing early, aren't you?' asked Gwen.

'Just got some shopping to do, but I'll get this paper out of your way,' I told her, grabbed a bundle and marched off through the sliding door, westwards.

'That's not where the rubbish goes,' Gwen shouted.

I ignored her.

I couldn't take the thirty-nine steps because at thirty-five I was at the wall of another house, number 24. How could the robber have counted to thirty-nine?

The supervisor, with the key to 24, had gone, so there was nothing else I could do that night, other than hop into an internet café and check Gwen's story. It was right! The police had arrested two men. There was talk of an accomplice, but he was never caught.

Next morning, I went to see the supervisor of the complex, and found 24 was for sale.

So, that afternoon, I got dressed and made myself up properly. I don't mind the overalls, but they're a bit bumfly, and it's always nice to feel feminine, and went to the estate agent's office.

As I walked in, Geoff said, 'Hello, you look charming. I hope I can help. You're the painter from 23, aren't you?'

I smiled, 'Yes, I am, and I was so taken with the complex that I wanted to find out about flat 24, which I understand is for sale. It's for my uncle Felix,' I said. Thankfully, he didn't seem interested in asking about any uncle Felix.

'It's one of the last built.' Geoff told me - which explained why Mr Robber had been able to get all his steps in.

'Why don't we go and look at it now, then maybe we can find a place to have coffee?' Geoff suggested.

'I'll think about the coffee,' I said, but the idea seemed attractive, Geoff wasn't actually good looking, more durable, strong chin, clear eyes, and I liked the way he sort of protected me as we walked out.

When we got into the flat, I paced out the sizes, for carpets and things I told Geoff.

Even then, I couldn't get the directions for the next leg of the map sorted out properly, and I didn't see how I would manage it.

We had coffee and Geoff asked if I knew that a famous bank robber had owned Gwen's flat. It came out so naturally; I didn't think about it. Then he mentioned the robber was fascinated by John Buchan, the man who wrote the spy story called The Thirty-Nine Steps, and I did wonder how he knew about that but said nothing.

Eventually, he said, 'You're a painter, and I've been having trouble selling number 24. Maybe, if you painted it, it would be more attractive, and if your uncle Felix buys it, it will be all fresh for him.'

I couldn't believe my luck!

I worked late to finish Gwen off and moved into the other flat two days later. I worked until it was getting dark, then stepped out the next thirty-nine steps - to a tree, according to the map. I stepped across the lawn and up to a boundary wall. There were still five steps to go, and when I looked over the wall, there was a road full of rush hour traffic. I thought about waiting until it died down, but I'd been working hard, and put it off till the next day. I wondered all night if I'd made a mistake, how could the next turning point be in the middle of a road?

I was busy painting 24, when Geoff came in and chatted for a while. 'I see they're busy with road works or something outside the boundary wall, the wall was put up when they made the new road last year. The wall's all right, but unfortunately, they took down several grand old oak trees when they made the road.' he mentioned as he left. He seemed to know quite a bit about the place, but he was the estate agent, after all.

I was so frustrated over the trees being cut, that I had a break. I went outside to look over the wall and lament over that old tree. My lamentations vanished when, low and behold, the road people had closed the road off with those red and white cones. Well! As you can imagine, I leap over the wall and had made those thirty-nine steps and the next, which were the last on the plan, in less time than it has taken to tell you about it.

After all the other disappointments, I suppose I should have expected something. Sure enough, when I got to the spot marked X, it put me in the middle of a fishpond.

They'll have dug up the loot when they put that in, I thought, and resigned myself to earning a living, when there was a lot of shouting in the road outside the wall.

I went to investigate, and there was a man, I took to be a foreman, explaining to a city gent that he hadn't put the cones out and closed the road, and didn't know who had!

As I was standing listening, Geoff came to join me, and we stood watching as the workmen collected the cone things and went off in a van.

When they'd gone, Geoff smiled. 'Forgot to invite you to the office party,' he said, 'I think you need a break; you've been working hard these last few days.'

After my disappointment over the fishpond, I thought, why not, he's nice enough, and I could do with some fun, so I smiled and said yes. He told me it was on Friday and was formal dress, took my address and said he'd pick me up at seven.

As he turned to go, he asked, 'What do you know about painting fishponds?'

'It's a different paint, but it goes on like any other kind,' I said.

'Maybe you'll be able to paint the one they're going to replace, I'll ask the manager for you, if you like?'

'Which fishpond?' I asked.

'There is only one,' he said. 'It's leaking, or something.'

'No job too small,' I told him. 'As long as the money's good.'

'I thought you might say that,' he answered, which I thought wasn't very chivalrous. I mean, it was him who wanted the thing painted.

For three days, I patched and frittered my time at 24, waiting while the workmen got the fishpond out of the ground, and the concrete base broken up, and it all loaded away. I nearly took a whip to them every time they had a smoke break, or stopped for tea.

The night they finished, I was in the middle of the hole with a spade. It took an hour of digging about before the spade hit something soft. I cleared the ground and pulled out a plastic bag.

The voice said, 'I'll take that.'

When I looked up, Gwen was holding out her hand and another woman had a torch and a gun pointed at me.

'Maybe we should shoot her here and drop her in the hole,' Gwen suggested.

'No, she has a date with me on Friday,' another voice said, and a searchlight came on.

As they led Gwen and her accomplice away, Geoff told me he wasn't really an estate agent, but an insurance investigator. They'd been suspicious Gwen was the unknown accomplice in the robbery but had no proof. When I came along, they thought I might be in on it, and let me work with the crooks, just in case - but Geoff said he'd never doubted me.

That put the writing on a very different wall.

thought left
dreaming screen
right **creative** typing
reading fiction **writing** plays essays re-reading
pen novel creating
re-writing **brain** paper
grammar science **editing**
drama

BARRY EAMES

I spent my working life, after graduating in electronic engineering, in the computer industry. I travelled the world living in both the USA and Australia. On retirement I studied Archaeology at Oxford University participating in many excavations and organising a society that discovered and excavated a Roman/Saxon settlement in south Warwickshire. My adventure into writing is recent, as an antidote to boredom brought about by 'covid' lockdown.

Portrait of a Painting

The Balance an M de Bono Property of a private owner

My art dealer Sharon [Fosse Gallery, Stowe on The Wold] vividly describes the first time she heard of Michael de Bono at the opening of the Summer Exhibition at the Royal Academy where she was introduced to a painting in the small western room. She describes the painting as a beautiful jewel like image of a young woman with a green headscarf set in a stark background. As I was going to the exhibition, she said I should look for the painting. When I saw it the intensity and technique of the painting felt like I was looking at a Vermeer.

Michael de Bono is a self-taught artist brought up in Wales. His paintings like the one I am featuring are often characterised by an emphasis on light effect and for reverence of the high Italian Renaissance and Caravaggio. This made him decide against a formal art education where he felt technical skill and art history were not valued. Michael's interest in the elegance and primacy of the natural world finds expression with his figurative subjects the intimacy of which invites us to reflect freely. De Bono adds "Art is made of flesh. All that I have done is in a humble way is to attempt to paint well and do a small amount of justice to the greats that inspire me".

The painting I am featuring not only reflects a richness and intensity of his love of some of history's finest painters but also the love of his model. "I love to paint, and I paint the woman that I love" he says "I like to communicate an optimistic message, one rooted in a life in which a peace predominates". This painting comes from a collection which he said was moulded by two separate instances the first by seeing Caravaggio's Supper at Emmaus and the second was learning of impressionist concept of colour. The painting 'The Balance' is an oil fourteen by ten inches on board. His love is the model. She is wearing a low-cut brocade dress, a blue woollen shawl over her right shoulder and a red headdress bunching her hair, and a teasing curl falls down her long elegant swan like white satin neck. A Renaissance woman? The lighting on her face and luminous white decolletage and the shadows are indescribable [truly a master]. Soft light through a window is on a globe of the world and a delicate balance is suspended from a thumb and fore finger of her lefthand. She looks serene and contemplative as though judging the balance of the globe. Did the artist have any symbolic meaning in his mind when composing the painting. I do not know.

The Balance
[A Painting by Michael de Bono]

Art reflects the artist's love of his model.
Beautiful jewel like image
Young woman.
Soft light through window
The sublime elegance of her profile

Graceful tilted swan like neck
Flawless alabaster complexion
Red lips playing a slight smile
Long soft lashes downward gaze
Luminous décollage shadows so quietly touching
Thoughts are drawn to Dutch masters
Impressionist colours.

Low cut brocade dress
Blue luxurious shawl over right shoulder
Blushing red head dress bunching her hair
Teasing curl down her snow-white neck
Renaissance lady.

With serene and contemplative air
Head tilting whilst fully gazing
As though judging for us
Globe of the world lit by the soft light.
Delicate long fingers tips suspend a balance scale
Perfectly balanced to measure to reassure.

Composition draws freely reflections
On his love of the great masters and his model.
Optimism and primacy of the natural world
Reflects in his figurative paintings.
A metaphor for a world on the edge?

The Eulogy for 'Athena Christiana' 1944-2019 Celebration at Chiesa di San Dominica Maggiore April 7pm.

Buona sera. Some of you may not know me, I am Marco, Athena Christiana's butler. I was her butler for more than forty years, prior to that a lover. She asked me to give the eulogy. She has participated in the composition as you would expect.

She died in her bed surrounded by her sons, two ex-husbands and ex-lovers. That morning her long time maid and dresser dressed her in her pink chiffon high collard negligee, applied fresh makeup, combed, and styled her hair. She looked serene, beautiful. As she passed away, she sipped from a glass of champagne. She instructed me how to order the service, who to invite and chose the music and hymns. She insisted that her white Persian cat Silviano was to be buried with her.

Athena grew up a 'scug Nizza' on the streets of Napoli, begging, singing for her supper. She was spotted by the great impresario Gregorio Carasini who paid for singing lessons. He moved her to school in Milan and gave her a name. She sang with the chorus at La Scala and soon graduated to an understudy. Her great break came when she was understudying to Maria Callasoni who couldn't go on because of a sore throat. Athena sang the part of Carmen in Bizet's Carmen. She was a sensation. As a member of the company at La Scala she was now singing minor roles. Athena and Gregorio were now lovers and he had ambitious plans for her. Over the next years she was to sing lead roles at Opera Houses around the world. The Met, Covent Garden, Glyndebourne, La Scala, Paris Opera, The Bolshoi. As a Diva she achieved world-wide fame. At the height of her fame the tragedy. Gregorio died from a heart attack. Heartbroken she retired to a solitary life with me her maid and Silviano on Elba. She was persuaded after two years to make a comeback by an old friend. She returned to rapturous acclaim singing Dona Elvira in Mozart's Don Giovanni at Covent Garden. She married three times had three sons and numerous lovers. Life with Athena was tempestuous and unpredictable more so as she got older. Athena retired from the stage twenty years ago. Her legacy is the 'Athena School' in Napoli. The school is for street urchins and orphans it provides food a home and education for the children on the streets of Napoli. Athena has left all her wealth to the foundation and the collection at the end of the service will go to the foundation. So please give generously. When you came in you were given a long stem red rose as you file out around the coffin would you please lay your rose on the coffin. As you leave the church you will hear Athena singing 'Exaltate Jubilate' [Mozart]. She wants us to celebrate her life not grieve.

Marco

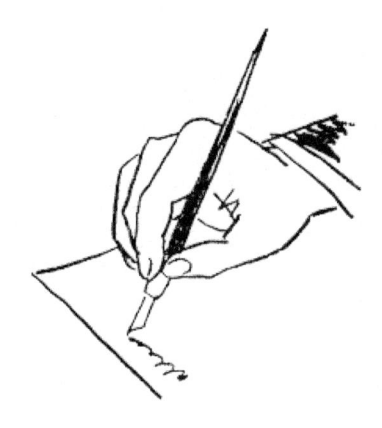

Robert Burton ...born 1577 – a Eulogy

Burton was a contemporary of William Shakespeare he lived during a period of much unrest in England, the plague, religious and political turmoil and the pending civil war. He lived at a period the seventeenth century which was rich vein of English literature.

He was born into a well-off land-owning family in Lindley, Leicestershire. He followed his elder brother an historian to Brasenose College Oxford. He matriculated aged 15 and transferred to Christchurch College. He was a fellow of Oxford University, and he obtained an MA and a DD degree and was librarian at Christchurch from 1624 until his death. He wrote plays only one of which survives and poems in Latin. One of his plays was performed before King James 1st on a visit to Oxford and apparently the King panned it. He obtained the living at St Thomas's in Oxford, his arms are over the church doorway and was rector of Seagrave.

His most famous work is the 'Anatomy of Melancholy' first published in 1621. The book is regarded as one of the greatest works of scholarship in the English language. He devoted his entire academic life to writing the book. Reprinted five times the final edition is 510,000 words. The

Weston Library of the Bodleian held an exhibition to celebrate four hundred years since the publication of the final edition from 29 September 2021 to April 2nd, 2022. Which I visited. Fascinating.

He writes under the pseudonym 'Democritus Junior, who was known as the laughing philosopher whose sole purpose in life was happiness.' The book is written in English and Latin. There are a great many quotations from contemporary, classical, renaissance and medieval writers. He explores the causes and symptoms and cures for melancholy like diet, digestion and sex and the more esoteric effects like love and religion he often attacks religious current teaching and practices. In attacking his subject he draws from all the known sciences of his day. He writes 'Know thyself is the subject of this book.'

Llewelyn Powys called it 'The greatest work prose of the greatest period of prose writing' and Dr Johnson reportedly said 'The only book that took him out of bed two hours earlier than he wished.' While a famous surgeon pronounced 'One of the greatest medical treatises.' He was a polymath a rare thing today in this world of specialisation.

There is debate whether or not he was a manic depressive, bipolar. By all accounts he was a jolly person. He would go down to the river at Folly Bridge and watch the bargemen and joke with them. He said that laughter as well as not being idle was a cure for melancholia.

> Void of sorrow void of fear
> Pleasing myself with phantasms sweet
> Methinks the time runs very fleet
> All my joys to this are folly
> Naught so sweet as melancholy.

The quotation is from one of his poems. Could this have been written by a manic depressive?

When he died in 1640, he left a library of at least 1700 titles. A very large collection for the time. The library he shared between the Bodleian and Christ Church College. Below his bust in Christchurch Cathedral is the inscription 'Known to few men unknown to even fewer here lies Democritus Junior for whom melancholy provided both life and death.'

The last six words in 'Anatomy of Melancholy'
'BE NOT SOLITARY BE NOT IDLE'

The Little Extras

I walked to the market square

'Good morning, Sietske, usual please hot chocolate and croissant.'

'Where's, Sue?' she asked.

'She has left me,'

'I am not surprised!' she said.

'So I have a vacancy for a carer do you know of anyone?'

'Not really but there is always Daisy May'

I sat on a bench in the square sipping my chocolate who should come by but Daisy May

'Howdee, Grandpa,'

'All the better for seeing you my, dear,' I replied.

She was dressed in skin-tight shorts a close-fitting red cropped sweater and very high heel shoes.

'Daisy May, I need a carer would you like to look after me?' I asked.

'Oww much?'

'100 pounds a week plus little extras!' I replied.

'Yer joking, Grandpa, yer knows I charges 100 a time!' she said.

'I know but you don't know what the little extras are, interviews will be in The Folly at 6pm on Tuesday'
Daisy May swaying clickity clacking tottered off.

Across the square I saw Albert approaching. He was limping dragging his left foot.
'Albert, why do you have a sock and shoe on your right foot, but your left foot is naked?' I asked.
'Because I can't find any left footed socks!' replied Albert.
'Why, Albert, can't you wear right footed socks on your left foot?'
'Because they don't fit!' he replied.
'Why don't they fit, Albert?'
'Can't you see my swollen big left toe?' he answered irritably.
I could it looked very ugly and swollen.
Albert, continued.
'I have two sock sizes M for my right foot and XXL for my left foot.'
'So you buy two pairs of socks to make one pair?' I asked.
'No,' said Albert 'I buy two pairs of socks to make two pairs, each pair is size M for my right foot and XXL for my left

foot, but I always have to buy two pairs at a time of the same pattern.'

'What is wrong with your left toe, Albert?' I asked …

'Gout!' was the reply.

'So how about shoes?' I asked Albert.

'I have to buy two pairs of shoes at a time size 8 for my right foot and size 11 for my left foot' he replied.

'Albert, is that why you often wear odd shoes?'

'Yes,' he said.

'What has happened to your left foot socks and shoes, Albert?' I asked …

'Greta, [his German wife] has burnt all my left foot socks,' said Albert …

'Why?' I asked.

'To stop me drinking at the Folly.'

'Why, Albert?'

'Because alcohol causes the Gout,' replied Albert.

Across the square we spotted a hunched back skinny figure with a large white bandage wound around his head approaching. It was Jack.

'Jack, what has happened to you?' I welcomed him.

'I have just come from the surgery,' he replied.

'Why, Jack,'

'Hilda, hit me over the head with a frying pan,' he replied.

'Oh dear. Why, Jack,' I asked.

'I called, her, a sow.'

Not a good idea.

'Why did you call, her, a sow, Jack,'

Jack and Hilda were the perfect characterisations for the 'Jack Sprat would eat no fat poem.'

'Because our bed collapsed under, her, enormous weight.' Jack replied.

'What did the doctor do, Jack,' I asked.

'He gave me a large whisky stopped the bleeding bound my head and said I should Sue for grievous bodily harm. He said, she, should get at least five years inside. I was on my way to the police station when I saw you lot.'

'Well well sit down, Jack, and let's all talk.'

I started:

'My wife has left me, Albert's, wife has burnt his left foot socks so he can't go to the Pub, Jack's, wife has pole-axed him with a frying pan and will probably go to prison. This is a case for man's liberation from female tyranny. The

solution is we all move into my house, and we hire a carer.'
Both, Albert, and, Jack, thought this was a great idea.

We met in The Folly Tuesday drinking Morland's Bitter and, Daisy May, toppled in.

'Large Gin and lime?' I asked.

'Thank yer, Grandpa,' she replied.

'Daisy, I should explain the caring job is now the three of us three hundred a week plus little extras' 'Cor not likely!' said Daisy May.

I gave, her, an envelope and said, 'Daisy May, before you make your final decision read the letter it lists the Little Extras.'

She read "Cor blimey, Guv, it's a deal!" she exclaimed.

'You have to wait for the sequel to find out what the little extras were.'

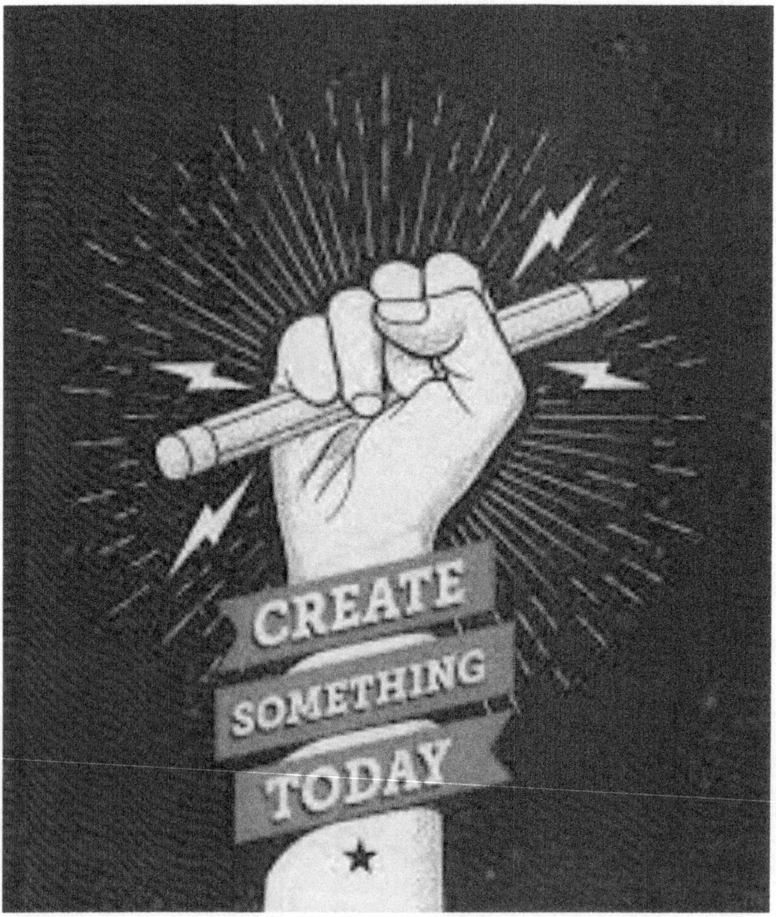
CREATE
SOMETHING
TODAY

VAL HUGHES

Writing has long been a passion. As a small child I would sit for hours writing and making my own books, trying to emulate the stories heard in school or those I had avidly read. Even now many years later my head is always full of poems and stories to tell so what better way to share that interest than to write a book or two. Writing can be a somewhat lonely interest and so belonging to a group of other like-minded individuals such as the Faringdon Writers is a real pleasure for me.

If you like my work, please pop to my website www.valhughes.co.uk for further information or like my Facebook page - Val Hughes Words & Art.

ENNUI by Walter Richard Sickert (1860 – 1942)

Property of The Ashmolean Museum Oxford

Ennui is the French word for boredom and this painting is said to describe the boredom of married life.

It depicts a Victorian dining room containing an older, lower middle-class couple. He is puffing contentedly on a cigar with a half-filled beer glass on the table. She stands behind him leaning discontentedly on a dresser, staring at a bell jar full of stuffed birds. On the wall behind her is a colourful painting of a younger woman in richly attired clothing, perhaps a singer or theatre performer. Despite the couple's close physical proximity, they each face in opposite directions, staring off into space. Sickert used real life models Hubby Hayes, an old school friend, and his ex-wife Marie, who often worked for him, in the painting, perhaps for a reason.

First painted by Sickert in 1913 at his house 15 Fitzroy St, London, it was inspired by a decayed first floor flat on the corner of Mornington Crescent which he also rented. There are five versions of this scene – two paintings and three etchings. The paintings are rendered in a post impressionistic style and were some of Sickert's later paintings.

Today the final painted version can be viewed in the Ashmolean Museum in Oxford - the original in the Tate Gallery in London. The Ashmolean version is considered by many as the more successful. It is smaller in size with brighter colours, patterned wallpaper, and a red rug tablecloth, replacing the dull walls and blank table in the other. The design is almost the same but here the bird cage and furniture feature less, with more emphasis placed on the people. Indeed, the smaller image creates an intensely claustrophobic atmosphere with the weight placed on the unsaid words between the two. The whole painting oozes a sense of boredom and dislocation. There is a sense of smugness in the man who has his home comforts, while the woman appears to have none. He is no longer interested in her or her feelings. In the words of Virginia Woolf *"it is all over with them, one feels. The accumulated weariness of innumerable days has discharged its burden over them"*. *

The marriage is seemingly suffocating with boredom, but it is left to us the viewer to supply the further narrative.

Sickert was a member of the Camden Town Group of artists and is considered by many to be the best English artist since Turner. Yet his work largely remains unknown. His earlier works are far darker and include 'The Camden Town Murders', a portrayal of Jack the Ripper's bedroom. Indeed, some of his paintings are so full of misogynistic views of women it boosted Patricia Cornwell's theory that Sickert was actually Jack the Ripper**.

This places an even more interesting perspective on the Ennui paintings and a visit to the Ashmolean Museum is highly recommended.

*Walter Sickert – A Conversation by Virginia Woolf
**Portrait of a Killer: Jack the Ripper Case Closed by Patricia Cornwell

Ennui

It is the heaviness of it

The dull unmoving

Permanence of its solidity

That bears me

Gone the colour

The animation

Like so many

Coloured feathers

Trapped in a vacuum

Neath a bell jar of repression

And respectability

I am there still behind that glass

It hangs on the wall

A memory of youth

A gewgaw trophy

Of your complicity

When did enough become turkey rugs

Glasses half full

Acknowledging the silence of the oak

Eulogy for Moses Buccanan – ol' Mose

"Hurrah for the Lord" were the last words Mose said
as he was laid on a mattress and set down his head.
Captured by white men at the sweet age of five
stripped from his family, sent off to thrive,
on a boat where men fought, barely staying alive
and from this great journey was blessed to survive.
Expected to understand many strange tongues
that sprang forth from the lungs of the most brutal crew
who were cruel and nasty, violent too.

Arriving in port, he was marched into town
and stood in a marketplace battered, low down.
A man stepped forward cupped his chin in his hands,
checked his ears and his teeth and removed his iron bands.
His life it was bought, his future, his keep.
He was put on a wagon with the cattle and sheep.

Arriving at a plantation, no friendly place,
Moses looked into the eyes of the cruel stranger's face.
Then his wife came to look and see what he'd bought.
"I got you a pet with which you can consort.

He's still a child so will need to be told,

how this place is run and his place in my world.

Make sure you don't ruin him keeping him soft,

or he'll bear the consequences, you'll see" he scoffed.

The mistress kept him her toy, a plaything, a trifle,

he slept by her bed, his closeness unrivalled.

She taught him to read, to write and to sing,

He brought her the joy she didn't get from her kin.

Eventually growing from boy into youth,

then handsome young man, rumours lofted the roof.

The Masser grew worried at what may have ensued,

took young buck Moses and him did abuse.

His beatings were frequent the lashings wrought bare,

the skin on his back, the curls of his hair.

Young Moses he prayed to the God up above,

asked for forgiveness for taking some love,

yet his hatred ran cold and burned deep inside

and very soon he decided to leave, run and hide.

He'd gone three days when caught by his foes,

they took him right back and cut off his toes.

A split through his nose meant all were aware,

he a run-away slave so beware, beware.

His walking was shackled, his head remained shaved.

He carried those scars with him full to his grave.

Moses worked in the fields and gathered his years,

with the others he helped through so many tears.

The cruelty of life did not pass him by

To say that it did would be a great lie,

Masser grew meaner with each passing year,

and cruelly killed, maimed, or tortured things Mose held dear.

But Mose piety grew, he preached of God's word,

to black and to white until he was heard.

Though starving and hungry, and worked hard and long

He never faltered in saying that man had done wrong,

Determined to care for his poor fellow slaves,

ease all their pain, and not create waves,

he ran into trouble again and again.

His kin oh they loved him begged for his life,

'til the day he was challenged and wounded by knife,

stabbed in the eye for looking too keen,

and lifting his head when bowed it should've been.

As the years advanced his respect it has grew

from a small boy of five until aged forty-two

Moses legend grown tall 'mongst the slaves in this county

and long are the tales of his goodness and bounty.

His mantra "God bless men them all, regardless of colour,

may they repent all their sins and love one another."

So, on hearing these words, the good Lord came along,

Gave Moses his peace and rewarded his song.

H G Wells 1866-1946 – a Eulogy

H G Wells is known as the Father of Science-Fiction. Born with a brilliant imagination he made himself famous by foreseeing the possible dangers of scientific progress as well as its potential to improve living conditions.

He was an advocate of 'free love' which he openly practiced throughout his life.

Always impatient for social change he pursued peace and global unity often quarrelling with the powers that be and was nicknamed 'The great awakener of men' by Clement Atlee.

Herbert George Wells was born on 21 September 1866 the youngest child of a small-time shopkeeper. Although his beginnings were humble, he became one of the most well-known men of his time. His childhood was very lonely, his mother prevented him from playing with the local children and his brothers were a lot older than him.

Wells was an exceptionally bright child but had to leave school aged 13 when his father's business collapsed. Over the next 3 years he found a variety of jobs including work as a teacher's aide.

It was at this time Wells found the joy of reading, devouring books in the school library, which sparked his imagination of other worlds and love of writing. After studying in his spare time, he won a scholarship to what is now Imperial College, gaining his degree in Zoology in 1890. While there he was taught by tutors including Thomas Huxley and Charles Darwin, leaders of the scientific revolution inspiring him and leading to his interest in social reform.

He wrote his first book aged 21 but was so unhappy with it he threw it into the fire determined to do better. At this time, he also fell in love with and married his cousin Isabel 'Mary' Wells. Wells however soon embarked on a series of affairs and one of these was his relationship with Catherine 'Jane' Robbins one of his students.

In 1887 he suffered a brain haemorrhage and was sent to Eastbourne to recuperate. Whilst there he had an article accepted for a local newspaper. Deciding this was a good omen he left Mary and set up house with Jane marrying her in 1895. A series of brilliant articles and short stories followed. He then wrote four of his most popular novels *The Time Machine, The Island of Dr Moreau, The Invisible Man and The War of the Worlds.* Science -fiction as we now know it was born. The public loved his work and demanded more and more. His theory that science had infinite possibilities for creating a better world helped him to continue imagining new worlds and new futures.

However, his health was not good, and following bouts of depression he suffered a nervous breakdown. The thought of an early death drove him to write more pushing the boundaries of what was considered then to be right and proper.

After the birth of two sons he lost interest with Jane sexually undertook yet more affairs. His interest in free sexual relationships, along with religion and science made him critical of Victorian morality. He wanted to do away with Victorian ethics claiming it would allow people to live a more fulfilling life. People loved his views of a bold new world of scientific progress but were not so happy to extend this to include sexual liberation.

He joined the Fabian Society (who promoted the restructuring of society) where he was challenged to a debate by George Bernard Shaw. Shaw declared him to be a dreamer of hollow visions. Wells, unlike Shaw, was not a good speaker and quickly lost the argument. He was soon asked to leave the Fabians when one of the member's daughters became pregnant. Wells ran away with her to France but soon decided she was not his intellectual equal and told her to leave but she did provide the material for his novel *Ann Veronica* about a free-spirited young woman who becomes a suffragette.

His publishers thought it too scandalous to publish, although his next novel *Mr Polly* had more success. The following book *New Machiavelli* also failed dismally with libraries who banned the book from their shelves.

One person who seemed to understand Wells views was the novelist, Rebecca West. They met in 1912 when he was aged 46 and she 19. The relationship soon produced a son, Anthony.

WWI was looming and Wells saw this as the promise of a new world order, his ideals coming true. He joined the Ministry of Propaganda coining the phrase 'The War that will end All Wars'. He was heartbroken when it turned into the slaughter of thousands of innocent young men and resigned his post immediately. Wishing to help world leaders realise the aim of a new peaceful world he wrote his ideas in the book *Outline of History* which sold 100,000 copies.

Wells was becoming a celebrity and was invited to go to the USA. Whilst there he had a fling with a woman who then tried to commit suicide in his flat. The incident soon dominated the front pages, placing his avantgarde private life open for all to read.
In 1920 he went to Russia to meet Lenin hoping to broker his ideas for world peace but despite his various political dealings Wells soon realised that his new world order would probably come to nothing. At the same time his rather complicated web of relationships started to fall apart.

In 1933 he wrote his book *The Shape of Things to Come* a prediction of the future which ends in 2106. And, not quite giving up, in 1934 he met with both Stalin and Roosevelt to try and find common ground on which to build a 'new world'. The outbreak of WWII saw the final collapse of his life's ideal and in 1945 one of his earliest fears about the misuse of science came true when the atomic bomb was dropped on Japan.

Although still writing, Wells was now living alone, without any companions or family, and desperately ill. He died alone on 13 August 1946, aged 79, of unspecified causes, leaving a note that his epitaph be, "I told you so. You damned fools."

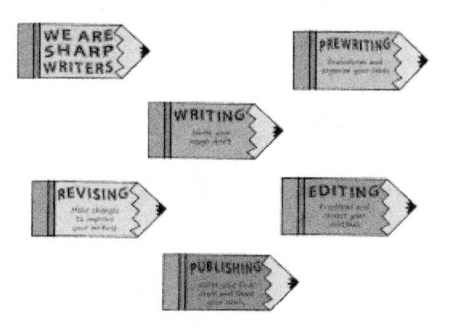

UFO Hunters

"So, something dropped from the sky did it? Is this more of your UFO nonsense?"

"No dad it really did, I promise, it really did happen. Just over there beyond the trees other side of Mr McGregor's field."

"Maybe it was Peter Rabbit!"

"I know you think I'm making it up but I'm not. If you come with me to look, you can see for yourself."

"Ok, but if this is a waste of time…I've had enough of your wild goose chases. I wish I hadn't shown you that UFO book I made as a child."

"Yeh Dad that was brill I've started my own. Mum gave me a new sketch book wanting me to be an artist so I'm putting all my UFO data and sightings into it and drawing what I see."

"Look I told you that was just a childish fantasy and UFOs aren't real. You do things as a child that seem very real but as you grow up you realise, they aren't. You're at the age now where you should understand that."

"I swear this thing must be a UFO like in the film Stardust…well she wasn't strictly a UFO she was a shooting star, but you get the idea."

"Are you listening to me? Urggh! This field is a boggy mess, I should have put my wellies on."

"Not far to the edge of the woods now though, and then we can track it. It should have made a big crater, or there'll be a fire ball, or…something."
"If something did happen as you say then I'm sure there would have been others who saw it and the police would be here by now."

"I didn't see anyone looking out of the windows only me. "
"Yes, but you wouldn't see people in houses further down the street on this side or even on the streets away further back."

"These trees are a bit scary in the night, aren't they? Lots of funny shapes. Dad! Dad! Do you hear that noise? A bit like a hissing sound, maybe its cannibal aliens."

"Ssshh! I'm trying to listen. I think it's coming from over there to the right. Can you see that faint glow? Quick, let's get over there…."

"Dad, the forest is very dark, and the trees are a bit thick over there. Do we have to go any closer? It might be better to wait, until the police arrive, from back by the road."

"Sssshh! Look there…you were right. Whatever it is has fallen into that pool of water hence the hissing sound. It's definitely not aliens in a UFO; I can see the Russian space agency symbol on it. More like a bit of one of their satellite launch rockets fallen back to earth. I'm surprised it hasn't burnt up on re-entry."

"What do you think Matt? Matt? Where are you? ….Some UFO hunter he's turned out to be!"

Who Shot Cock Robin?

Detective Sergeant Harry Hardcastle looked down. The blood from the chest of the corpse made a flower shape on the green and blue linoleum floor of the back room. "Better check he's dead."

Nodding, his fingers on the carotid pulse, the constable said, "Been some while as well. The body's cold."

"I'll get a message to Scotland Yard. They'll want to be kept up to date – mystery shooting an' all that. As if we haven't enough goin' on in this damn Blitz."

Another constable entered from the front of the pub. "Looks like there's been a wedding sir. Sign on the board, Congratulations to Denny & Francis. Plates and stuff all over, looks like they didn't have time to tidy up, must have been the air raid. Some tasty cake left though – took a lot of rations to bake that one."

"That'll be Denny Watkins & Francis Collins, heard the bans read last week," said Hardcastle lifting the body slightly. "Bit of a Spiv that Denny. Not sure what Francis sees in him. A nice young lady, nice family…. Been shot in the chest at close range, powder burns on his shirt."

Holding his notebook he walked into the front bar looking for clues amongst the remains of the party. Hardcastle knew the Collins' family, they worked at the local farm so could get eggs and other hard to come by supplies which probably explained the fruit cake. A rare treat, rationing made any cake-making difficult; his wife was always telling him. He lifted the cardboard and rice paper cover, picked up a small piece of cake, and popped it in his mouth.

"Find out who the guests were," he said brushing crumbs from his tie. "We need to interview everyone present, see if they have any information for us. Who found the body?"

"Local air raid warden – came in 'cos the street door was open and light escaping."

"No sign of a struggle sir just a broken glass, killer must have surprised him."

"Or been someone he knew."

Turning, Hardcastle's foot collided with something which skidded across the floor. "Wait a minute, what have we here?" He bent, took out his handkerchief, and carefully picked up a revolver. "Dropped it on his way out no doubt."

"Looks like we found the murder weapon then."

"Maybe. See what the ballistics and print boys have to say first."

"Looks like army issue."

"Oh Christ…. that means Military Police," sighed Hardcastle, "that complicates things."

~~~~~~~~~~

Hardcastle waited. The Military Police arrived quickly, all rules and regulations.

"We'll take over from here then, as it's army business," they said, pushing everyone aside.

"And I'll need to see some identification first," said Hardcastle, "this is our case until proven otherwise." Satisfied, he handed over the gun. "It hasn't been dusted yet. You might want to get that done first. Victim is Robin Edwards. Landlord here at The Fighting Cock. Bit of a miscreant we've had our eye on him for while…. black market smuggling, but nothing to pin him down. Not surprised he's ended up like this."

The soldier looked at him dismissively and focussed on the gun which made Hardcastle bristle.

"Yep, this is an Enfield No.2 standard issue, made locally - Royal Small Arms factory just round the corner. Interesting. No worries we'll check the serial number, see who's missing their side-arm. It's an offence to use or carry arms for non-military purposes."

"Or maybe we have a thief at the factory. Now that would be a real issue," said the other MP.

Hardcastle shook his head as he walked away. "I'm the local man these parts. If you want to know more about the people involved – let me know."

He was duly ignored and bristled again. This was a murder inquiry why did the army have to see everything from their own point of view. He left them to it having organised for the body to be collected and next of kin informed.

~~~~~~~~~~

Sergeant William Collins lay on the bed his head thumping. The wedding had gone well but he couldn't remember how he got to his cousin's house, or what had happened after the last couple of brandy's. He didn't know where Robin had got it from, but the brandy toasts were much appreciated. However, having outstayed his chit he would now be considered as AWOL back at the barracks. He did not want to think about what might happen. In the worst-case scenario, he could be court martialled, sentenced to 2 years.

His rank could be removed, his pay stopped or if he returned quickly, he could return to his unit and be dealt with by the CO who might just apply a field punishment. It was all dependent on how quickly he could get back to camp. Fingers crossed they would want him back on active duty – he was, after all, being posted overseas in four days' time. Better get moving he thought dressing. He was just putting his boots on when there came a loud banging at the front door. "Military Police! Open up at once!".

Will's heart began to thump. How did they find him so quickly. If he could only get back to the barracks before them. He didn't stop to think but slid open the bedroom window and climbed out, shinning down the drainpipe as he had done many times as a child, and ran.

It was only after he stopped to catch his breath, he realised his holster felt light. He shouldn't have had the gun with him anyway. All small arms were supposed to be checked in on exiting the camp for leave. He only did it to impress Mary Finn. He would have to go back, maybe it had fallen out and was on the floor or under the bed. Checking there were no MP's in the vicinity, Will entered the house as he had left it. Frantically searching the room he could find no trace of the weapon. He lifted the mattress at the same time as his cousin came through the door brandishing a poker.

"God, mate you gave me the willies. Wot you doing back here? They've only just left."

"Looking for my gun, I can't go back to camp without it."

"Don't worry about the gun," his cousin Pat said. "They've already found it."

Will brushed his hand through his hair. "I'm done for now then - AWOL and losing my weapon." "

"Worse than that mate, they found it next to a dead body at the pub. Came here looking for you, you're a suspected murderer."

Will felt all the blood drain from his head into his feet. "But I never killed anyone – Did I?" His cousin looked as blank as his mind felt.

"I know we were very drunk but even so you'd remember something like that wouldn't you. Who am I supposed to have killed?"

~~~~~~~~~~~

Having learned about Robin Edwards Will set off to see Francis. See what she suggested, she always knew what was best.

The streets were littered with the rubble from the previous night's bombing and the house Francis and Denny shared had no windows left. Skirting the front of the building Will entered the back garden where he thankfully saw Francis talking to Denny, or so he assumed.

He stumbled on the remains of the kitchen window. Francis turned his way at the sound of breaking glass, and he caught sight of Det. Sergeant Hardcastle. He looked to run but then thought against it -it would only look bad.

"Hold on son," said Hardcastle "don't do anything silly." Will had known Hardcastle all his life. "Don't worry Sarg I won't."

"Tell me what happened," Hardcastle said coming closer. "I don't know I was very drunk, woke up in Pat's house, knew I was AWOL and tried to scarper back to barracks quick like when I realised me gun was missing. So went back for it only to find out I was wanted for murder. I don't remember killing anyone. Didn't even know who it was until Pat told me what the MP's said. They out looking for me?"

"Possibly not right now more worried about the gun. Are you sure nothing happened between you and Mr Edwards?"

"Not that I can remember."

Francis shuffled and made to go into the shell of her house.

"Where's Denny?" Said Will.

"Taken to hospital, deep cuts to his back, neck and arms. Threw himself over me to save me from it and then got caught himself. There was so much blood."

"Do you know anything Fran?" Will said.

Hardcastle waited with a cocked ear.

"No. Just telling Sarg we came home after the first sirens went off, to be private like, instead of going to the public shelter. Denny went into the garden to get the Nissen hut ready. He was a while but came back just as the bombs started dropping nearby and threw me to the ground, fell on top of me as the windows blew out."

How long was Denny gone said Hardcastle getting out his notebook.

"About twenty minutes I think."

"Mmmmn.... interesting. Was everything OK during the reception between Mr Edwards and Denny?"

Francis shuffled her feet "I...I think so. They had a bit of a row at one point, but Denny said it had been sorted." Her face reddened. "Robin said Denny owed him for the food and booze and as we had no money left to pay, he would take first rights with me instead." She explained they had shouted at each other a bit more, but then the air raid siren went off and everyone left the pub.

Hardcastle wrote something in his notebook. Putting handcuffs on Will the pair walked three streets down to the police station which was still standing. You'll have to stay here until I've sorted this out, he said to Will and left him in the cell.

~~~~~~~~~~~~

Arriving at the hospital Hardcastle was told Denny Watkins was in a bad way. The glass had caused lacerations to his neck, and he'd lost a lot of blood. They were doing their best to keep him stable but could not guarantee what happened. His wife had been notified and was on her way.

The doctors said he could speak to him for a few moments but if the wound started bleeding again, he would be sent packing. A nurse would stay with them just in case.

Denny didn't look too good - laying on his front, his back and one side of his face and neck heavily bandaged.

"Hello Denny," said Hardcastle. "Can you tell me what happened last night after the air raid warning went off."

Denny sighed and screwed up his face. He knew he was on limited time you could see it in his eyes.

"I owed him money he said, lots of money for black market goods I sell on me stall and the wedding. He wanted paying and said he would… Francis…." he faltered and tried to wipe his nose on the back of his bandaged hand.

"I know," said Hardcastle, "she heard it all. I need to ask you officially. Did you kill Robin Edwards?"

There was a moments silence.

"Yes," said Denny.

"Can I ask how?"

Denny went on to say that he'd gone back to the pub after pretending to get the Nissen hut ready for Francis. He didn't intend to kill Robin but wanted to finish the conversation. Denny found Wills gun on the table where he and Pat had been sitting drinking brandies. He picked it up for protection. Robin was in the back room, he got angry and smashed the sampling glass on top of a barrel coming towards Denny with it shouting 'let's see if she likes the look of you after this'. Without thinking he pointed the revolver and pulled the trigger. Seeing what he had done he dropped the gun and ran back through the bar and out through the side door. He ran all the way back to Francis just as the air raid started proper. One bomb was coming in close and finding Francis in the garden on her way to the hut he threw her to the ground. Then he was covered in shards of glass and wood ending up here. He hoped the pub would be destroyed and no one would be the wiser. Ironic really. Red had started to seep through the bandage around Denny's neck. The nurse shouted and rang the bell for assistance asking Hardcastle to leave as Francis burst through the door. She ran to Denny and buried her head in his hair as he lost consciousness for the last time.

~~~~~~~~

Having been released by Hardcastle Will was accompanied back to the barracks and handed himself in to the CO. He handed over the letter Hardcastle had given him explaining why he was unable to return to barracks on time but was proven innocent of the charge. The Military Police were unhappy that their case had not materialised as expected although had instead made a big deal about the gun. Sentenced to 2 years suspended sentence for illegal use of a military weapon and no promotion Will joined his fellow soldiers and boarded the plane for action.

SCHARLIE MEEUWS

I am a grandmother who moved 15 years ago from Oxford to Faringdon, where in the summer months I dedicate myself to our garden; on darker days I create photographic designs on the computer, but my main passion has always been poetry. From writing my first poems in my native German I moved on to later writing in Spanish, French and finally in English. I prefer simple vocabulary. What fascinates me, are the possibilities to express emotions. I love poems that seem small on the page but swell in the mind.

Eulogy for a Poet

Without digressions and steadily
You grew old like a river reaching the sea.

As one who reaches the sea and the sand,
you let go off the safety of the land.

You fought the storms battling with age.
Your spirit overcame. You turned a page.

Your words became salty and filled with shells,
drifting in light and drafted in spells.

Young in its fervour, brother of the waves,
your heart carried weight, wherever it braved.

Wherever it braved, you came into being
as when morning dawns and night is fleeing

in the slimmest of lights, and you suddenly know
a new day is born, and you feel aglow.

You reached old age undisturbed by chance
with time for reflection and eager for balance,

with a gift to listen, repent and find peace,
as the sea waves receive, hold on and release.

As the sea winds play with an errant dove
may the Great Spirit enfold you with love,

carry you, written in wind, salt and sea
to Elysium's infinite harmony.

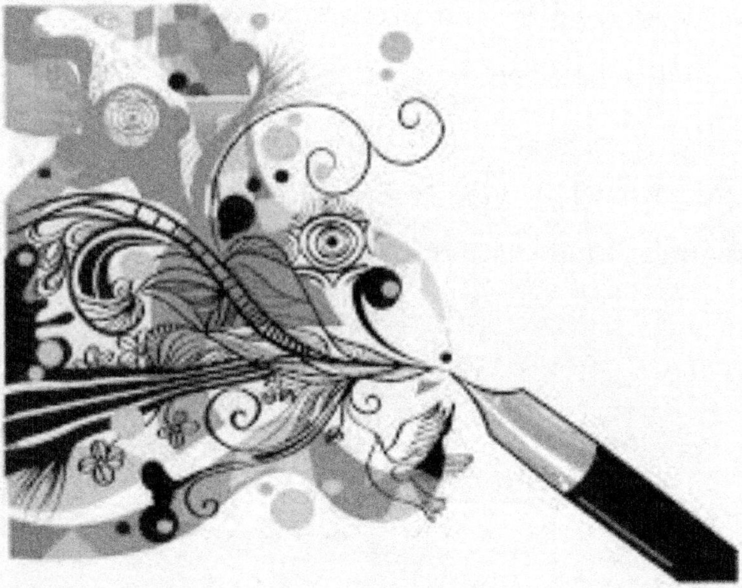

DIANA MOORE

Diana has been writing since she was nine years old. She received her first prize, a watch from *Bunty* magazine for writing witty book titles.

Word play and humour come naturally to Diana, and she has since had comedy sketches performed in the Oxford Playhouse, a short comedy drama about Henry VIII in Oxfordshire Theatres, (nominated for originality of writing), humorous (sometimes serious) poems presented live to audiences visiting the Ashmolean Museum, and a Lottery Funded theatre production for adults with dyslexia.
In the process she has published three illustrated poetry books which are used in her creative writing and poetry performance workshops for children and adults.

Books: Objects in the Ashmolean, An Art and Poetry Resource / A Visitor to the Forest, a scripted poem designed for performance / A Fishy Coat Tale and Other Poems, humorous poetry book.
For further information and enquiries please visit:
www.diana-moore.com

Winter Scene by Gustave Courbet

Jean Désiré Gustave Courbet
Gallery 66 The Ashmolean Museum, Oxford

And this is the place of my childhood

Barren, bumpy, bare

branches to be explored

To climb, to swing,

To swing from

My legs roughen and bleed in that copse

And there's a secret

Shhh!

Snow will melt

The ram, the torso

Shadows and shapes

Do you see them?

Do you see the shape of my childhood?

That house

Over the way

The one on the end

It's empty now

He went away

I skip and slip across the bumpy mounds

I was happy

I was sad

I am a
writer.

I create.

SAM TINDALE

I have lived in Uffington for more than ten years, but I grew up in the Norfolk countryside where I fell in love with fairy tales and the poems of Walter De La Mare. I've taken a long path to writing, but now I write in my garden office every day, where views of the Ridgeway compete for my attention. This year I have been revising my second draft of a contemporary psychological thriller and have completed the Undergraduate Diploma in Creative Writing at Oxford University. I joined the Faringdon Writers Group in 2019 and continue to be amazed at how many different ways a simple prompt can be interpreted! I enjoyed writing the pieces for this anthology and look forward to new writing projects in 2023.

Me and My Parrots – Frida Kahlo (1941)

Inspired by Mark Twain's description of a woman as being '… the kind of person that keeps a parrot', I hunted on the internet for paintings of women with parrots – and discovered Frida Kahlo.

I expect you might feel a vague familiarity with Kahlo's work – the vivid Mexican colours, her flamboyant traditional costumes, and the powerful gaze reaching out of her many self-portraits – but this painting represents an unexpected oasis of calm in her severely painful life. Kahlo has painted herself seated with only her upper body visible. The scene is a brief moment of peace with her four pet parrots, one on each shoulder and two secured in place at her waist by her hands which gently rest on her lap. Each of the parrots is actively looking in different directions to Kahlo, and their feathers are ruffled. Each of them looks restless, ready to fly away, which contrasts with the stillness of the artist in her short-sleeved white blouse. Kahlo has captured the parrots' splendid feathers in such shimmering detail that it's impossible to believe the parrots are almost invisible in the painting – but the longer you stare at the painting, the deeper Kahlo stares back at you, challenging you, challenging the world. You can't quite meet her gaze, so you focus on the uncompromising details of her thick eyebrows and the dark sprinkle of facial hair across her upper lip, before you finally realise, she's a beautiful woman with an unrelenting jawline and perfectly rouged lips. You cannot tell that her loose blouse is a disguise to hide her spinal support devices, just as you cannot see that the long traditional skirt hides her withered right leg.

A victim of childhood polio and then critically injured at eighteen in a bus accident, Kahlo spent many years of her life in unremitting pain, trussed in spinal supports and corsets. Her right leg was shorter than her left, she was subjected to many operations, (including having her lower right leg amputated), and was frequently housebound. But although the pain was hard to bear, Kahlo loved, and was loved, with passion and turmoil, throughout her life. Although so bound to the artist Diego Rivero that she married him twice, Kahlo had many lovers, male and female, and she lived the life she wanted to live, supporting the communist and nationalist causes she believed in.

Me and My Parrots was painted shortly after her Father's death and her return to Mexico to live in the Casa Azul, her childhood home, with Rivero. Kahlo died in 1954, after a bout of pneumonia, and Rivero arranged for her home to become a museum which remains open today in Mexico City. But, if you want to see this mesmerising painting, you will have to content yourself with reproductions because the original sold for $130m in 2021 to a private buyer – and is now lost to public view.

Me and my parrots by Frida Kahlo Property of a private buyer

Me and My Parrots

Do you see me
as you stare at my face –
the face I wear to face you?
Do you see the pain behind my lips
the lips I blood to distract you?
Do you think I'm peaceful
with talons in my flesh
with beating hearts trapped in my arms
with feathers whispering flight
whispering escape?
Does my beauty make you forget
my steel cage
my clipped limbs
my murdered heart?
Do you believe you see me
when it is I who see you
as you stare at me and my parrots?

Eulogy – Miss Sylvia Brown

One, or both, of my parents would have been standing here, to remember their beloved friend Miss Brown, if they had been able to attend today. In their place, I am honoured to have this opportunity to say goodbye to Miss Brown, my childhood neighbour, whom I have always thought best described by Mark Twain's endearing quote as being '… the kind of person that keeps a parrot.'

My parents lived next door to Miss Brown for almost fifty years, but although I only lived there until I left home for university, I saw her every day of my childhood, either waving good morning from her kitchen window or peering at me from behind her spectacular rose bushes – her pride and joy. Woe betide any of us kids who got caught leaning over her wall to pluck those roses to make sticky cups of sickly-sweet brown perfume that we sold for 10p to our long-suffering parents. We never, ever, made the mistake of trying to sell it to Miss Brown.

Miss Brown, Sylvia – as she *never* asked me to call her, was already retired when I was old enough to understand what that meant, but if my parents hadn't told me she had been a teacher, I would have known from her forthright, take no-nonsense manner – and from her efficient kindness displayed in the blackouts of the 3-day weeks. Miss Brown had a gas cooker! And that meant feasts of beans and toast by paraffin lamp at her kitchen table. It's only now that I wonder what my parents ate – Miss Brown only ever fed the kids… And she was as generous with her hobbies as she was with her baked beans. Her hands were always busy with knitting or crocheting or painting. And then there was the pottery. Hmm… Let's just say that I still have the beautiful blanket she crocheted for me, but there are none of her mugs in my cupboard!

I know that Sylvia, (because if I cannot say her name now – when can I?) volunteered as a teacher all over the world, because she told me the stories behind the African masks on her walls and the brightly striped South American poncho she always wore to go to the shops, the one that looked like it had been stolen from a llama. But, never one to miss an opportunity for good, she encouraged me to think about the school children in other countries, children without roller skates and calculators, children without running water, children without food.

I am so grateful that I had the chance to thank Sylvia for my life in education, for my travels to distant lands – and for my love of gas cookers. In that final week of her long hospital-stay, I stood in awe by her bedside.

'Close your mouth', she said. As if I was still five years old.

But it was hard to close my mouth when faced with so many cards. So many that the nurses had put up string across the walls, to hang them like Christmas cards. Cards from every school, every class she had ever taught. Cards from Nigeria, from Chile, from Malawi. And, from her later years, cards from her neighbours, from her fellow knitters, and, yes, there were cards from the potters. 'Read them,' she commanded. And I did. I read the words from all the other children she had educated, guided – and inspired. Not just me. Hundreds of us. We are Miss Brown's achievements – living our lives beyond her years.

My card stood on the bedside table, a print of Frida Kahlo's 'Me and my parrots.' It's a self-portrait of the artist, stern-faced in a white blouse with two parrots perched on her shoulders and two parrots held against her chest.

Sylvia looked at me and smiled.

'I think I would have liked to have been a person who kept parrots,' she said.

And like everything else about Miss Sylvia Brown, her parrots would have been as unforgettable, and as inspirational as her, (and probably better at pottery).

Robert A. Heinlein (1907-1988) – A Eulogy

I believe that the science fiction novels of four-time Hugo Award Winner Robert A Heinlein are the first adult books I fell in love with. Yes, I had read books by HG Wells and John Wyndham, but I had watched too many black and white films for their books to reach my heart. Heinlein was different. Covering deep social, political and cultural themes with a deliberately racially diverse cast of intelligent, self-driven male AND female protagonists, his books opened my eyes to a future where space travel was simply an every-day fact and love, in many, many forms, was worth living for.

As a science nerd in the early 80's, with the ever-present threat of nuclear annihilation curtailing my expectations of a long life, Heinlein's novels were an introduction to what is now known as 'hard-science'. Heinlein's background as a Naval engineer, and his marriage to a chemical engineer, Ginny Gerstenfeld in 1948, ensured that he paid meticulous attention to the veracity and plausibility of the science in his novels. This raised his stories above the level of 'pulp fiction' and Heinlein himself invented the phrase 'speculative fiction' to separate his writing from traditional science fiction. Today, the term is used more widely to cover the broad spectrum of writing that includes elements that do not exist in reality, including fantasy, horror and science fiction. Ginny was Heinlein's third wife and is believed to be the main influence behind Heinlein's strong female characters, particularly the title character in *Friday* (1982), one of my favourite adventure books of all time. *Friday* is set on earth, at a time when continents are run by mega-corporations rather than governments – a situation that feels credible at a time of Apple, Amazon, Facebook and Elon Musk.

Unusually for today's speculative fiction, most of Heinlein's books were stand-alone stories until a series of repeat characters entered into his later books, with mixed critical reception – his writing awards were all for his earlier works. His first widely successful novel *Starship Troopers* (1959), also controversial, was written in response to increasing demands to stop nuclear testing (although Heinlein fans, including me, are critical of Paul Verhoeven's film which only carries Heinlein's title, not the story). Heinlein is best known for *Stranger in a Strange Land* (1961), which tells the story of how a human, Smith, raised by Martians on Mars, returns to a post-war earth where organised religions are politically powerful. Controversial, because of the free-love aspects of the invented religion, it became the first Science Fiction novel to enter the NY Times Book Review's best seller list.

As a writer, Heinlein was committed to supporting other science fiction writers, including Ray Bradbury, and he freely offered writing advice to anyone who asked. He regularly quoted his five rules of writing:

1. You must write
2. You must finish what you write
3. You must refrain from rewriting, except to editorial order
4. You must put your story on the market
5. You must keep it on the market until it has sold.

Heinlein's works were always controversial, particularly his exploration of free love, and sexual taboos such as incest, but his intent was to provoke readers into questioning sexual norms rather than the promotion of any particular agenda. It is probably the critical response to this aspect of his novels, and the establishment of a religion called The Church of All Worlds, loosely based on the religion of the same name in *Stranger in a Strange Land*, that prevented me from shouting out on a daily basis how much I loved Heinlein's novels. But, through having done this small piece of research, I now know that Heinlein was never directly involved in the invented religion – and it has since been disbanded. My love for Heinlein is renewed! And I am now going to read *Farnham's Freehold* (1964), one of his classics that I seem to have missed out on – and then I'll reread another favourite *Time Enough for Love* (1973). I can't wait to get started....

Getting Rid of the Rubbish

2010
"Why are you doing the bin? I told you I would do it!"
"Yes, but when will you do it, David?"
"When it's full."
"It was full two days ago. Can't you smell it?"
"Oh, that's what that smell is. I thought it was the cat."
"Well, I've got my shoes on, so I'll just take it out now."
"No, no. I told you I would do it."
"Too late. I'm doing it now."
Front door slams.

2013
"Can you do the bin today?"
"Bin! Always with the bloody bin."
"Well you did say you would do the bin."
"Yes…. I know."
"You told me that you would do all of the horrible jobs."
"Yes. I know I did…."
"So, will you do the bin today please?"
"Yes. Of course…."
"When?"
"Later."

"Later when?"

"Later, later."

"Oh fuck it, I'll just do it now."

"No, I said I'd do it!"

"Well do it then."

"I will. Later."

"I'm going to take it out now."

"I said I would do it."

"Too late, I'm doing it!"

"Stop it!"

"No, David, I won't 'stop it'!"

"Put that fucking bin down!"

"No, I'm going to take it out."

"PUT. IT. DOWN."

"No. I'm taking it now!"

Front door slams.

2015
"The bin smells."

.....

"Can't you smell it?"

.....

"It must be that fish wrapper from Tuesday. It's foul."

....

"I can't sit here, with that smell."

.....

"Where are you going?"

"*I told you. I can't take the smell.*"

"What smell?"

"*The fucking bin stinks!*"

"OK, OK. So you want me to put the bin out? Just say so!"

"*Well, it doesn't make any difference when I do ask you to.*"

"You never ask me. You just passive-aggressively whine about it."

....

"So, now you're going to sulk about it."

....

"What are you doing?"

"*I'm taking the bin out.*"

"Put it down."

"*No.*"

"Put it down!"

"*No. I am taking the bin.*"

"*I'm* taking the bin."

"*You never fucking take the bin.*"

"I always empty the bin."

"*When?*"

"Always!"

"*So, David, just when exactly did you last take the bin out?*"

"Last week."

"No you didn't."

"Yes, I did."

"NO. YOU. FUCKING. DIDN'T!"

"I did."

"Well, I'm taking it out now."

"No you're not!"

"Yes, I am. Just watch me."

Front door slams.

2017

"It's rubbish collection day today."

....

"I said, 'it's rubbish collection day today'."

....

"Alright, alright. I'll take the rubbish out."

"Thank you, David."

Front door slams.

2018

"I've put the bin out."

....

"I said, 'I've put the bin out'."

....

"I heard you."

"Well you could have said something."

"Like what?"

"Like, 'Thank-you'."

"For what, David? For doing what you said you'd do for the last ten years?"

"Yes. For that. For that – and everything else I do."

"Do you really want to start comparing who does what in this house?"

....

"Because I have a very long list!"

....

"Well, do you really want to start this argument?"
Front door slams.

****

2020

"It's rubbish collection day today."

"I know. That's why I've already taken the bin out."

"Great, thanks Phil."

ELLIOT VANDERHYDE

I am an Oxonian poet who works in search and rescue as a full-time first-response technician. A passionate enthuse who has been writing since primary education when authors like Korky Paul, Roald Dahl and Spike Milligan were visitors to the kinder-blackboard. I view poetry as a constantly improving piece of art, however, rather than left of the brain there are patterns of imagery and scansion or rhythm which are technically definitive within my portfolio. I have explored music and been showcased on BBC radio Oxford music introducing. I am a facilitator alumnus with the National Youth Theatre of Great Britain, a fantastic UK charity. I am not least excited to get my second pamphlet printed about Faringdon countryside called 'Green Belt Gnotches'.
Elliot Vanderhyde offers self-published material on www.elliotvanderhyde.com.

The Windmill by Vincent van Gogh

Le Moulin de la Galette 1866 Private Collection

This wind.

Am I a slave to its breezes?

When something blows out my fire

Till empty at all, then a quiet still drawl

I will never surrender nor fall

People know me

But I'm no wonder

I'm a work of poetry

A Crime Story

The land is visible by full moonlight, let on by our mizzenmast lookout shouting and pointing at his spotting ahead. There is no need for alarm because yonder red herrings have been reported, above the sea's swell about 3 miles but they are often actually cresting waves. Rogue but serious enough that the swift water breaks over the deck. Washing a mist that murkies our misdirection like undiagnosed tuberculosis coughing up chaos, or the mortal flailing of a newborn babe. To our heart's relief the Flannan Isles are eyes on, yet, without any assistance from the Northern Lighthouse Board.

We are a trading vessel sailing from Philadelphia to bring emergency hospital equipment across the pond to Scotland during peacetime. The date is 1900 the year of our Lord.

Reaching port today and our ship's doctor; who is chosen and a well-informed man, recommended that we sail for the gannets that encircle the Outer Hebrides, to navigate through small submerged rocks that might damage the hull. We've rotated to alleviate invisible threats; we're on a direct course to the mainland, lest we run aground; but it will be a week by my estimate before my log is acted upon. When the board will understand that we have been utterly neglected by the lighthouse crew of the Flannan Isles, thus our survival depends solely on the Anchtor and her mariners' nautical expertise.

"A steamer vessel carrying sponges was the sum of my view, however, innermost thoughts, which I would have kept private to the ears of my fellow man, would have restrained if it wasn't for the impertinence of the American captain. I told him that a hirelings welfare at sea should be expected to be impoverished when they are destined for over 2 weeks of travail. I said to the right honourable captain of Hesperus; I do care little for the history of a crew's mission when it differs so greatly from the remittance of my grade of remuneration," shares Robert Muirhead to newspapers, before gathering his investigators to meet the island; 3 days after the complaint is received, he leaves the isle of Lewis.

Laden with relief for the lighthouse, the Hesperus anchors down. Firing flares and sounding a foghorn, but there is no orderly response from the islands, and no flag is hoisted to welcome them. Take an oar and row and find out more.

Rocks that shimmer like mirrors dispel us,
Clock hands that splash in delirium compel us.
The welfare of men, the fellowship of plinth keepers
Rue them who have slayed all their gallantry to sleepers
If slimy steps outstretch like a carpet of sin
Would these of the walkway show an air of my kin?
For the Hope for the guide for the light and the truncheon.
Boarding we'll find them, the Hesperus shall hunt them.

"Unlock that door", Buckland's green eyes bulge in breaching, for he should find signs of life behind the unlogged wooden supply boxes. They are also rotted through to their contents, and they pass by this until one of the company sees the door if it is a door, because it's unlocked and ajar.

Familiar with the captain's birthday, Buckland Darran involves himself much in the backstage life of the ship, he had recently made a cake not too long before. He remembers covering the prickles of his wiry hair in a tied-back ponytail to stop the evolution of tiny hair follicles falling into the mixing bowl. Being too small to spot for his ageing eyes; which are like that of a swampy toad.

"My crew's eyes were swathed with grief and anchored to the earth; they thought about their wives and young children. Joy had failed them, having eyes on, also meant that the lost crew were just that, when we looked deeper into their quarters." Logs Robert the captain of the Hesperus.

Unsatisfied with the unexplained absence of his employees. Captain Muirhead does not abandon the night's stay with the relief persons. He communicates by a lantern with Hesperus offshore. He commands the crew to begin rinsing the mercury through a cloth and spinning the prisms that statue on the precipice. At history they signify 2 oilskin coats missing and one remaining, which leads to furthermore suspicions when half-eaten meals are found lotted about; an up-turned chair like someone had been fighting; clean and replenished oil-lamps; Christmas cards shelved festively like a petting zoo; the watch of the night was ticking at the centre when they found crew's logbook. That is when they heard the icy gasp that echoed down the column hollow of the hall.

*Shout! *

Reading the crew's log, December's second week shows reports of the affairs of the crew in the same handwriting in turn. Recording in the last entry that certain persons were thought to be hardened and historically violent brawlers, complaining with tears. And most spine-crawling; our denial of a storm they had recorded as the worst they had ever encountered in twenty years as keeper.

Parting the glass; the prism of the past.
The ocean 'neath humans and his belly that gasps

Morning comes, and Robert has the words penned in his diary. Professionally, the Northern Lighthouse Board investigation officer writes his questions down about the shouting noise and reassures the others of the rationale of unpredictable winds that draft about the uppermost of the keep. But even Robert himself admitted it sounded like a talking voice.

Whereas the relief crew is duty-bound to stay. Robert, however, responds having no systematic resolution to the question of the lighthouse crew's disappearance. Secretly, for the first time in Robert's life, he remembers the countenance of his American colleagues to be of substance. Undermining his father's house being British-born and consistently resentful of the colonial cause. There was a baseline emerging, to acknowledge the least integrity because of the reports being made by the steamship; had they not done so with such diligence, the families of the keepers could have all been left in the dark.

Robert, with the lighthouse crew, agreed upon a declarative document to which every man subjected themselves. Naming it themselves to be entitled 'the constitution of Flannan Isle'. Robert Muirhead shares his condor moment, before eating breakfast and they pray a declaration; for the peace of the families. Making the investigation into the welfare of the crew in subjection to the goodly authority of the living God. Christian's praying leads to the dismantling of the equipment outside, in the rotting boxes, food, a flare gun and oil for the lanterns.

Robert signals the Hesperus, and a boat then arrives shortly expectantly.

"Relax; we didn't find them. Calmly, restore this letter to the hand of the Lighthouse Board. I'm staying", says Robert. That was when the rowing boat left, and Robert chases the steps back, he covers his hat to prevent the peak from kiting away.

The impossible isle that beats our heids for the while
When duty-bound keepers are abandoned for bile
Gross misconduct dismissal life be but a kiss all
What crown binds our story and gives God his acquittal

A boy is washed in the swell is what happened my heart tells
their great coffin acts swiftly to take quickly to fell
No rumours and debating that my eyes may see courts
How have poor lives been taken or deemed worthy of abort?

Standing on the aisle, Captain watches the Hesperus come away to prevent her risk in the turbulent sea as the wailing wind talks voices, putting evil over the mission with razor blades of laughter. That is when the rest of the crew complaining about the captain taking long, calls him inside.

"Captain Muirhead! Captain!" They shout. Robert steps towards the edge of the plateau. He turns, "The voice," Robert says. "A boy's voice, can you not speak of it?". Taking action the crew drag Robert into the keep before a wave sweeps him of the violence of a man attacking him where he placed his feet a moment before.

Where needed, the limping cat that the relief crew brings to the party coughs meaning approximately that the animal is sick or there is something licked by its tongue partially blocking the airway.

"Maybe you should have gone back to the Hessy." Says a familiar voice.
"Buckland", Robert reassures after he catches his breath.

After an evening passes, the first watch of the night means that someone is supposed to get eyes on the prisms at the top of the stairs. Robert looks up the column of stairs to check and there is one above; the lamp is switched on but it's unmoving. Robert ascends the flight of stairs as fast as humanly possible since the issue makes sailors at high risk in a volatile region. The higher up one is the stairs the more you can sense the weather. In the premier set, Robert is mindful of what the crew must face for months at sea, isolated, separated by miles. At the top of the bell, the mercury is contaminated with thick mud and dust from the sediment of the seabed. The Voice of a boy speaks louder and louder with screams.

*Shout! * *Shout! *

Robert focuses on his breathing, the veteran mariner knows he needs to stay calm, get warm and finish his investigation of the crew. Robert makes the lighthouse rotate on its cogs and paces down the column, he smells the pungent chemical in the air.

Suddenly, the voice makes more sense, the word that is annoying Robert isn't murdered it's- mercury! That is when Robert notes down that it might have been what was distressing the crew because Mercury is a highly toxic liquid metal that can cause delirium and it is hallucinogenic. Ordinarily, Robert files his notes before taking action but this time he pushes to the mess and admonishes the relief crew with extreme causticity.

Toned by wrath which the captain stirs, the argument ensues contrary to how gentlemen ought to refer to one another at the turn of the 20th century. Buckland calls Robert a filthy tyrant to his face, Captain Muirhead calls to engage in a legal settlement, and he walks into his bed-chamber when SLAP! Sackcloth violently smothers over his chin. Breathing through the material, causes the fibres to rub up against the captain's throat and lungs. The crewmen hog-tie him and uncover the mask, Robert is relieved with oxygen after the suffocating experience.

After a winding punch to his side, "That's enough." Says Buckland receding the violence.

"Question; dear old friend. How could you allow grown men with families, with years of living to be exposed to that stuff?"

"With ease, I was hoping for an early Christmas."
"Early. That's what the old crew wrote in the logs?"
"I will report the findings to the proper authorities, don't do this."

"Don't he say?" Buckland looks at the others who crease up cynically. "No, you feel that rope, Captain Muirhead. That rope burns, ooh but you still think you are in charge. Twist the knot."

"AHH!" Robert shouts.
"Right here, right here. You see, Rob. I'm in charge now...and your orders are to sit tight"

The door slams and a chair is jammed behind forsaking the captain leaving him in the dark, icy air for a minute; Captain Robert only hears the sound of a drip drip-drop when water falls from the stalking pipes. That's when the door screeches open, two burly crew holding the frame letting Buckland in with a hammer.

"Present arms." Says Buckland.

Buckland thinks the lighthouse board is just a figment of the imagination, boiling with the envy and disappointment that the turbulent sea could never imitate because of an expectation out of waiting. "This filter you use to strain the mercury is called normal technical procedure." He says.

"Strongly stated, poorly educated." Spits Robert in reply, with the blood from a cut venially oozing down his face.

Buckland brandishes his bludgeon, "Present."

PETER WEBSTER

Although born in Cambridge, Peter has lived in Faringdon for nearly forty years now. As a long serving member of Faringdon Dramatic Society, he has so far written eleven pantomimes which have all been premiered in Faringdon as well as being presented by other societies, including one in New Zealand! In addition to his pantomimes, he has also written several one act plays, one of which, 'Nighthawks', went on to win the Oxfordshire Drama Network One Act Play Competition 2013. Having spent so much time writing plays, trying his hand at stories and poetry has been a real challenge!

A Study of Loneliness?

There aren't many paintings that would inspire me to write a play, but Edward Hopper's 'Nighthawks' did exactly that.

Hopper, was an American naturalist painter, a resident of New York; it took many years before he made his breakthrough as an artist, but when he did, he made quite an impression – but he certainly wasn't an impressionist! His paintings seem to express many things – loneliness, regret, boredom, isolation, resignation; that makes them sound depressing, but that could not be further from the truth. Every painting tells a story.

He painted 'Nighthawks', probably his most famous work, in late 1941. What do we have in the image? Very little, just four people in a New York diner; it looks late, but there's no clock, so we don't know how late. There's no visible door to the diner – they appear to be 'locked in'. So, what's going on here? Hopper isn't saying – he leaves it to the viewer to work things out and to write their own scenario. Who are these people – what's going on in their lives and heads? What's happened to leave them looking as they do?
Was Hopper depicting the loneliness of a big city, where you get lost in the numbers? Was he showing the breakdown of a

relationship – are the man and woman drifting apart? When you look at Hopper's 'actors', they can seem cold and hard; but maybe they've lost everything they believe in and are in their very own 'prison', totally disconnected.

Just how alone is it possible to feel?

Note: Edward Hopper was born in 1882 and died in 1967. My one-act play, inspired by this painting, (and also titled 'Nighthawks') deals with the lead up to, and the aftermath of, the attack on Pearl Harbor in 1941, the same year 'Nighthawks' was painted.

Thoughts on Nighthawks.

Through the glass, four unknown people

Inside their mental goldfish bowl;

Between each one a virtual wall,

Despite the purpose of the place.

Within the image, no track of time

Beyond the feeling – late at night.

Out of the image, such loneliness,

Across the years, a sense of pain.

Behind their eyes such unread thoughts,

Outside perhaps our own experience.

From the image a conjured story,

Within the grasp of Hopper's mind.

A Eulogy

Welcome; welcome to you all, his many, many, relations gathered here today to remember our friend; and welcome also to just a few of his admirers from around the world. It's been ninety-six years since he came into our lives, but his presence has been such that it feels that he is still with us and will never, ever, leave.

It may seem strange, but I almost feel that I have to apologise for what I am going to say – how can anyone have lived such an apparently blameless life and to have been loved by so many? My answer to that, is that during his life, no one has ever had reason to say a bad word about him. But has he been a saint? Hardly; but more of that later, for who can forget his doomed adventures?

So, in almost the words of the Bard, I come not to bury him, but to praise him – which I can only think of as a joyful task, as he has truly been the salt of the earth and loved by more people than he can ever have known. He has always been utterly loyal and has never been heard to utter a cross word – there are very few of us who could make that claim to fame! Perhaps that explains why he has made so many friends, from every walk of life and in many countries. That, in turn, shows why his work has been translated into so many languages.

He's earned a reputation for always doing things his way and never, ever, taking the obvious or logical route; sometimes, of course, that has led to unlooked for consequences, something else he has been loved for. Life, people, and sometimes creatures have often been a mystery to him – many a time he's been puzzled by others' motives and actions, usually taking a considerable time to think them through and to decide on a reply, if indeed a reply was needed. Modestly, he's always put down any failure of his to understand a situation, as being due to having 'very little brain'.

At times, that lack of understanding has made him underestimate his true worth; others have never made that mistake as they know he has been nothing but kindness itself. He's always been generous to a fault, and that generosity has applied especially to birthdays, although it must be said that sometimes his choice of a present has fallen rather flat and not always been appreciated. Mind you, he's never given anything that he hasn't already tried himself, and usually in advance!

For once I have to strike a discordant note, as there was a time when some Australian immigrants arrived in the neighbourhood and he was one of those who at first resented their presence and tried to dissuade them from settling; however, he very soon saw the error of his ways and from then on actively welcomed them. That natural kindness also applied to his love of animals; I am sure you're all aware of the work he has done in finding homes for animals, especially donkeys. Even more worthy has been his use of recycled materials in that context.

And who can forget his bravery? There was the time, when at great risk to himself and in considerable discomfort, he set out in a makeshift boat to rescue a friend trapped by floodwater; he was so successful in this endeavour that during a party held in his honour, he was presented with a medal for his courage. And then there was also the occasion when he helped rescue a creature stuck high in a tree and afraid to climb down.

I promised to touch on some of his 'doomed adventures', for in his so very varied adventuring I think we have to agree that sometimes he was rather bound to fail. For instance, when he discovered a bees' nest high in a tree, he decided that he must help himself to their honey, something he was extremely fond of; but when his attempt to climb the tree failed, rather than risk tumbling into a gorse bush once again, he decided, much to everyone's amusement, that he would reach the nest by balloon. Not only could he not reach the nest, but neither could he return to earth until the balloon was punctured by a well-aimed shot.

And, of course, there was the time he and a friend decided to track an unknown animal in the snow. They spent ages going round and round in circles as the tracks multiplied, but they never did find what made them. Then, in an attempt to increase scientific knowledge, he spent time studying the diet of big cats in captivity; as part of this study, he decided to attempt to trap wildlife in the forest, but only succeeded in falling into his own trap and having to be rescued. Last but not least, there was the expedition in search of the North Pole, dogged by bad planning, too many participants and the very rapid consumption of provisions; an endeavour not helped by his inability to navigate in foggy conditions.

It cannot be helped, but when talking about him, we do have to mention his struggle with his weight; such as the time, when visiting a friend, he ate so much that he became stuck in their doorway when he made to leave and had to stay wedged there for a week. But at least he lent a hand, (or should I say leg) with the washing!

Finally, I must mention his flair for poetry; he was justifiably very proud of his rhymes, hums, and songs; so, let's remember one of his best. It goes like this:

Cottleston, Cottleston, Cottleston Pie,

A fly can't bird, but a bird can fly,

Ask me a riddle and I reply

Cottleston, Cottleston, Cottleston Pie.

Cottleston, Cottleston, Cottleston Pie,

A fish can't whistle, and neither can I.

Ask me a riddle and I reply:

Cottleston, Cottleston, Cottleston Pie.

Cottleston, Cottleston, Cottleston Pie,

Why does a chicken, I don't know why.

Ask me a riddle and I reply:

Cottleston, Cottleston, Cottleston Pie.

So, let us think of him as if he is still with us and will never leave us; known and loved by so many, the world over. And, of course, we can't forget his finest achievement, the invention of that great game, now universally known as 'Poohsticks'.

Thank you.

James Boswell – a Eulogy.

James Boswell – a man who, to say the least, led a very full life. Was he a libertine or a master of his craft? The answer is simple – he was both, something we should be grateful for, as his experiences lent much colour to his writing.

He was born in 1740 in Edinburgh, the son of Alexander Boswell, a judge, who was later to become Lord Auchinleck. James initially studied law, but in 1760 he ran away to London, where he was taken up by his father's friends and where he sowed his wild oats. He had decided on a career in the army, but when nothing came of it, he returned home, living a dissipated existence but passing his Civil Law exam in 1762.

By 1763 he was back in London where, once again, he failed to obtain an army commission; however, it was then that he met Samuel Johnson, he of dictionary fame. This was probably the most important meeting of Boswell's life. Having been told by his father to find a proper career – if not the army, then in law or politics – James pursued none of these, but with Samuel's encouragement set about recording his rather dubious lifestyle in the book now known as 'The London Journal'. The diary he kept over a nine-month period is an intimate account (sometimes very intimate), of his encounters with both high and low life; frank and confessional, 'The Journal' is also a vivid account of eighteenth - century London, a forerunner perhaps of that kept by Samuel Pepys.

In 1763 James completed his law studies in Utrecht, Holland, and then set off on his own Grand Tour, travelling widely in France, Germany, Switzerland, Italy, and Corsica; it was during these travels that he met such luminaries as Jean-Jacques Rousseau and Voltaire. Once back in England in 1766 he recorded his experiences in his private papers, those titled 'Boswell in Holland' and 'Boswell on the Grand Tour'; by all accounts he had once again left a trail of broken hearts in his wake.

Then came a sort of settling down; James was admitted to the Scottish Bar, becoming an advocate for seventeen years, and in 1769 marrying his cousin, Lady Margaret Montgomerie; he still made regular visits to London, where he built a circle of friends which included Richard Brinsley Sheridan, David Garrick, John Wilkes, Joshua Reynolds, Oliver Goldsmith, and Edmund Burke.

In 1773 he finally succeeded in persuading Samuel Johnson to join him on their celebrated tour, which he recorded in 'The Journal of a Tour to the Hebrides', which came out in 1785, a year after Johnson's death. In yet another change of direction he took on the publishing of 'The London Magazine' from 1777 to 1783, writing a series of seventy essays under the pseudonym 'The Hypochondriac; in the meantime, he succeeded to the Auchinleck estate. Boswell then moved his legal practice to London, only to find that his skills were not in demand; however, this gave him the time to start work on his masterpiece, 'The Life of Samuel Johnson', which was published in 1791 and is generally regarded as one of the finest biographies in the English language.

James spent his last years in London, his wife having moved back to Auchinleck for her health; he had hoped to be asked to undertake political work, seemingly not realising his true vocation – that of a writer. He was still his old self – restless, debauched, but popular and excellent company, hence the circles he moved in. He died in May 1795, after a short illness, his manuscripts only coming to light in the late 1920s.

James Boswell, an artist, a born journalist, and researcher – maybe not read widely in this day and age, but well worth seeking out. I think I need to reread his London Journal!

Is That all There Is?

It is late at night; two people are talking.

"A penny for them."

"What?"

"I said 'a penny for them'; you were miles away."

"Was I? I'm sorry."

"Don't be – you've obviously got something on your mind. Come on, out with it."

"It's nothing, nothing at all; don't mind me."

"No, come on; something's eating you. Whatever it is, let it out."

(There is a silence.) "You won't understand."

"Well of course I won't if you don't tell me. Look, whatever it is, you need to get it off your chest; it can't be that bad."

"Alright, if I must; I've been having a think about us, about you and me...."

(Jumping in.) "What d'you mean, 'you and me'? What about us?"

(A pause, then:) "Hell's teeth! I knew this was a mistake – I'm sorry I started. *(Then more angrily.)* You never once stop and listen, do you? For God's sake! Just once!"

"No, sorry, sorry, you're right! I promise I'll keep quiet. Go on."

"Like I said, I've been having a think about us, what we do and where we're going. We've been together for so long, it's like we're taking each other for granted. We love each other – at least I think we do; we get along fine, and we don't seem to argue – not much anyway. But that can't be all there is? At least, I hope not." *(Another pause.)*

(Baffled.) "I just don't get where you're coming from right now, or what on earth's brought this mood on. What more do you want for Christ's sake? We've both got good jobs, so there's money coming in; we've got a pretty nice house in an okay area, and we've got each other. What more do you want?"

"What more do I want? What sort of question is that? Listen to yourself! Is that really <u>all</u> you want out of life? What about hopes and dreams? You must have some, somewhere in that head of yours."

(Losing patience.) "Oh, come on! Be a bit realistic, can't you? You can't live on hopes and dreams – talk about airy-fairy! You'll be booking a retreat next!"

"Well, maybe I just should – at least I'd get some thinking time to myself! *(A pause.)* Look, I don't want to argue – that's just what I was afraid of. You're so bloody practical – that's good, but sometimes, just sometimes, it's just too – I don't know – limiting! You're right, we've got all the comforts of home, but don't you sometimes want to break out of that damned comfort zone? *(A pause.)* Well, don't you?"

(Another pause; then exasperated:) "I honestly haven't a bloody clue what you're on about! Yes, I'm practical – just as well one of us is! So, go on, enlighten me, what've I got to do to get out of my so-called comfort zone? So far, I haven't the foggiest where you're coming from. What more do you want, I'd like to know? What more is there?"

"What more is there? What sort of daft question is that? If you haven't got it by now, you'll never get it, no matter what I say. I'm not sure I know you anymore, or if I ever did come to that."

"Go on then, try me! Can't be that complicated."

"Alright then, I will! It's like you and me are stuck in our very own goldfish bowl, swimming round and round, never getting anywhere. Never branching out! *(A pause, then, with emphasis:)* There are new people I have to meet, new places to go; new things to try, new experiences I have to have. Even, heaven help me, new books I have to read…."

(Butting in:) Is that what all this is about? Is that it? Really? We can do all of that, if that's what you want. I just need to get online, make some calls, make a few bookings. Problem solved!"

(More silence, then quietly:) You really don't get it, do you? You haven't and you never will. I'm going to do all those things, believe me, I will. But – I'll be doing them by myself from now on, because I'm climbing out of that effing goldfish bowl. You can have it all to yourself. Enjoy."

(The sound of conversation fades away.)

Forgery is a Fine Art

What a view! I ask you, what could be better than a warm night, a cold beer, the sound of waves on the sand and someone to talk to? What a country this is, just beautiful. Coming here was certainly the right choice; whatever happens there's no way I'm going back, that's for sure. Why did I come here? 'Cos I've been a rather bad boy, that's why. Oh, there's no great mystery to it, but you could say I've had to do a bit of a runner. Relax! I promise you I'm harmless! Just to be really clear and before you start to worry, I haven't hurt a soul – well maybe just a little bit, but I only hurt them in the pocket. I can live with that!

What've I done? Let me have a think. You're sure you want to know? Okay then, get me another beer and I'll tell you – but no names, right? So, let's see; where to start? Well, all you need to know about me, is that I'm an artist for my sins – and no, I'm not famous, that's the problem. I'm not bragging, but I've got talent; I can draw, and I can paint, but my work just doesn't sell, at least, not for a sensible price. Maybe people think it's derivative or they just don't get the subject – who knows? So, no sales means no cash coming in;

one way or another I've burnt through all the cash my family's built up, going back years.

So, I have a good long think about what to do; no way am I going to get some dead-end sales or office job, about all I reckon I'm fit for. Then the light dawns; if I can't sell my work, I can damn well sell someone else's – not as a dealer, oh no, I'll indulge in a little harmless forgery! There's no end of dodgy stuff out there already, a load of it on the walls of major galleries; and that just proves that there are plenty of very gullible, so-called experts and collectors out there, just waiting to be conned. And even if I get caught, there'll be little risk, going on past trials; maybe a fine and a short sentence. Even better, no violence needed, only persuasion. The only weapons, pencils, and brushes!

But, and it's a big but – whose work to forge? What subject and what materials? Well, for a start, the artist has obviously got to be dead; on top of that, any work needs to be rare, hardly ever coming up for sale. So, I go through a great long list in my head; Turner, Seurat, Gainsborough, Hals – and a whole lot more. Whose work can I best knock off, and enjoy doing it? That's crucial, the enjoyment's got to show. But then something strikes me – how in God's name do I get the materials? The right ones for the period? One mistake and I'd be on a loser. Not only that, but the authentic stuff costs a fortune, money I don't have.

Then I get the answer, obvious really. I won't be doing a painting, just a preliminary drawing; but it would have to be one for a really well-known painting. It won't have the same value as a painting of course, but it would still be worth a small fortune if I can pull it off. So, then I start researching these drawings and discover that there isn't a single one attributed to Vermeer. Not only are his paintings very few and far between, but drawings are non-existent! One of his paintings got sold for sixteen million not long ago, so if my drawing gets taken for genuine, that's going to make a killing. It's dead risky 'cos, like I said, there's no record of any Vermeer drawing, but I reckon it's worth a try. If it comes off, I'm on a winner!

So, I decide to come up with a preliminary for a Vermeer, but which one? I do a few quick sketches of a few of his paintings, just to see what I'm up against. In the end, it's blindingly obvious which one I'm going to work on, no discussion needed. It has to be that one everyone knows as

'The Girl with the Pearl Earring' – don't know why it took me so long to see it.

So, that's the subject decided, but what's the story behind it? How the hell would I have come by it? Whatever it is, it's got to be convincing. Then it comes to me, and as a cover story it doesn't get much better; I remember that one of my dim-distant ancestors really was trading in Holland in the sixteen-hundreds, so I can say that that drawing's been in my family for centuries. But then, how did we come by it? Whatever tale I come up with has got to be believable. Well, how about this? Maybe the Dutch merchant who owns it, is still owed money by people who've lost theirs in the Tulip Fever crash; and let's say that it catches up with him in the sixteen-sixties, when The Pearl Earring is painted, and he finally runs out of cash. And then to pay off his outstanding debts, he gives it to my ancestor, and that's how it ends up here. Impossible to prove or disprove, but I reckon it would stand up.

So, that's the plan – Mr Vermeer is going to make my fortune, but to do that, someone has to buy my drawing, but who? No way will it be easy; auction houses and galleries will be likely to ask a lot of awkward questions, and to be annoyingly suspicious. They'll have probably been taken for a ride before. No, what I need to do, is to find a private collector, who might be tempted to take it off my hands; maybe someone keeping a low profile while sitting on a pile of dirty money. Someone who's rather keen on building up his own private gallery, and then keeping it all to himself. I say 'he' because that sort is almost always a 'he'. And then, of course, I realise that I don't know a soul who fits that particular bill; not surprising really. A bit of careful, very unobtrusive, research is needed, and I have to tread very softly, very softly; indeed, so, I park that problem and set about getting the drawing done – otherwise this was all just words.

So, first things first; I need the paper to draw on, and that means the real stuff – paper made in the sixteen-hundreds. Not only does it have to look the part, but any prospective buyer might just decide to have it dated, so it has to be the real thing. I need large sheets of paper, two or three to be on the safe side. The solution? Blank pages from some book of the right period. But where the hell am I going to find them? I think about the obvious, like the V and A or The British Museum, but I reckon they'd be too damned hot on security; no, what I need is somewhere where they might be just a little bit more relaxed. Somewhere like a college, an old established one, 'The Dreaming Spires'.

So, I take a trip to Cambridge, timing it for one of those open days when they let you have a wander round, and do a circuit of some libraries, ending up in a nice quiet one. What I need is a book, the right age, the right size, with those blank pages – and I can't take long to find one, or someone's going to get suspicious. After a few minutes I find just what I'm looking for – a great tome by some anatomist, dated sixteen twenty-one. Ideal. Then when the librarian gets waylaid by another visitor and they go off on a search, I get my craft knife and cut out all the blank pages I can find and slip them inside my coat. Then I put the book back and get out as quickly and quietly as I can. That's the one thing I feel guilty about – spoiling that book, but needs must.

As soon as I get back to base, I set about producing that drawing, otherwise what's the point? Practice makes perfect, so I don't touch the pages I've nicked, apart from roughening up the cut edges and checking they're about the right size for a Vermeer - and they're almost spot-on, talk about luck. So, I start to do a whole load of practice runs, so many I lose count, until Vermeer's lines are second nature.

The final drawing mustn't look copied, it has to look 'free' – like it's been done before the painting, not after. When I think I've finally nailed the image, I go for the real thing – and the second attempt is a winner! I've got it dead on – Vermeer couldn't have done better! I've managed to get that girls' expression exactly – that slightly tempting, slightly erotic, half smile; I make a few changes though, this is supposed to be a preliminary drawing after all. I make her earring oval, not round, give her some longer eyelashes, and that's it. What I don't do is sign or date it – I'll let the buyer decide who drew it!

So far, so good; I have something to sell, but a buyer is nowhere in sight; I need someone with cash coming out of their ears, but no traceable source of the cash. And, what d'you know? London's full of people like that! So, I start reading the serious papers, looking for the big players and who owns those mansions in Chelsea and Hampstead; only trouble is, it seems they're all owned by offshore companies, dodging tax. So, then I go to the society pages; who's doing all the charity work and who owns all the racehorses? Nothing. And then I do what I should have done right from the start – I look up who's been spending big money at

Bonhams and Christies? Who's been buying the Warhols and Bacons?

The more I look, the more one name crops up – and that's a name you don't want or need to know. So, the next question is, how on God's earth do I get close enough to make a sale? I need someone on the inside, otherwise no chance. So, I began staking out this mansion on Bishops Avenue, watching who goes in and out; and I spot this guy who turns up at the same time every evening and leaves the same time every morning, so he's obviously on the staff. And the way he's built, I reckon he's something in security, maybe a bodyguard. Like that song, 'He's six foot four and full of muscle'. I've got to get close to him, he's my passport to his boss – so I follow him when he leaves one morning. He doesn't go home, wherever that is, but goes into this posh coffee shop and sits down at one of the stools facing the street. It's now or never, so I go in, order a coffee, and sit down as close to him as I dare.

Somehow, I have to break the silence, so I say to the world at large, "This is the life – nothing to do but watch the world go by". And he sort of smiles and says, "Alright for you, but some of us have to work for a living". I tell him that I'm between jobs right now and ask him what he does, keeping it as light as I can, just for conversation. He's a bit tight lipped, but he let's on that 'he advises people on security'; so, then I said, "What, like advising people how to protect their Picassos"? And he says, "Something like that". Then as jokingly as I can I drop in, "Maybe I should talk to you about my pride and joy then"? And before he can say anything, I show him the photo of my Vermeer drawing. He takes my phone and I see his eyes light up; he tells me he thinks it's beautiful and asks can he have a copy? I say something like, 'only too happy, help yourself'; and then I watch as he downloads the image and then gives me back my phone. By now, my coffee's finished, so I tell him to have a good day and to enjoy the picture, and then I leave him to it. With luck, I might have sown the seed; pretty soon it turns out, that's just what I've done.

And two days later, I get the call I've been hoping for; it's the guy I'd spoken to in the café, telling me he's shown the picture to his boss, who's a collector and wants to know if I'll show him the original; I tell him I'd be delighted, only too happy to share what gives me so much pleasure. The next thing I know, I'm sitting in that mansion, drinking some very expensive champagne, regaling my host with the tale of how the drawing came into my family and where it's been all this time, and why it might be a genuine Vermeer though I can't prove it. I tell him his eyes will show him if I'm right. It's only then I unpack it and let him take it to the light.

He stands looking at it for what seems a very long time, though it's probably just a minute or two. Eventually, he turns to me and says he's got to have it, and how much do I want for it? And I tell him that it's not for sale, that I can't sell something that's been in my family for generations and gives me so much pleasure. Then he makes me an offer, and it's more than I'll ever earn in my life, but I still refuse; he offers even more, and I sit for a while letting him stew. Then I say I need to think about it, pack up the drawing and leave, hoping I've made the right move.

And it seems that, just for once, I have, 'cos the very next day I get a call, asking if I've made a decision and reminding me of just how much cash could be coming my way. I let him sweat for a bit, and then say, yes, I'll go for it, but only because the money will let me build the place I've always wanted and maybe get married someday. So, that's the deal and I've played it straight all along. I am who I said I am, so the cash goes into my account. Mind you, it doesn't stay there long; I do just what he would've done - I put it 'offshore' double quick, and now I'm offshore myself! And if he ever decides it's a forgery, I'll claim that I was taken in just like everyone else; as they say - 'Let the buyer beware'.

And that's the story. You've listened to me for quite long enough, so It's time I bought you another beer – I think I can afford it!

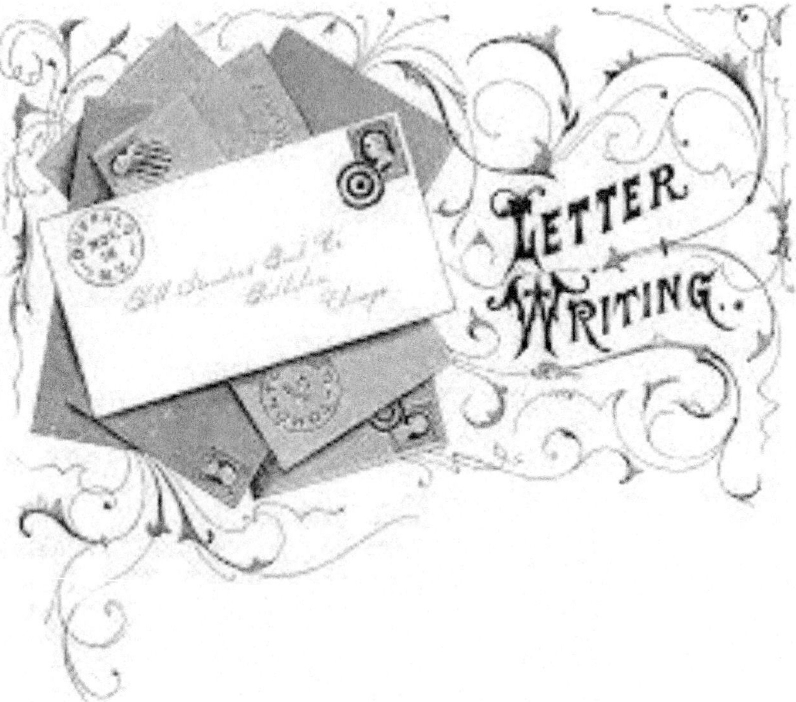
LETTER
WRITING..

JOCELYN WISHART

Jocelyn retired a few years ago from science teacher training at the University of Bristol where she led several research studies into teaching with new technologies including Smartphones. She and her husband then moved to Lechlade to live closer to the River Thames where they keep their narrowboat. She is currently enjoying the challenge of Creative Writing with the Fairford branch of the U3A as well as with the Faringdon Writers Group though she hasn't yet managed to get her novel reimagining the life of Anne Bonney, the pirate, into publication. Recently, her poem 'Birth of an Island' was selected as one of the top three winners in the national U3A's 2022 Poetry Competition.

Movement in Squares by Bridget Riley

Bridget Riley was working as an illustrator for a graphic design company in the late 1950s when, having studied pointillism including the work of Georges Seurat in detail, she began to explore art further but as an optical science. For several years she focused on how creating black and white geometric patterns can produce illusions of movement even colour. This work wasn't always popular, many visitors at her exhibitions reported feeling seasick yet today she is known worldwide as one of the founders of the Op-art Movement. Her iconic picture 'Movement in Squares' was painted in emulsion on board in 1961.

The painting itself originally resulted from a sketch where Bridget had been colouring in alternate black squares as she pondered on what could be found in a square. As she shaded more squares, she noticed that the squares began to lose their original form creating a three-dimensional effect that continuously changed even as you looked at it.

These days those familiar with the widely published work of the neuropsychologist Richard Gregory can quickly explain these visual effects as the brain using its learned experience

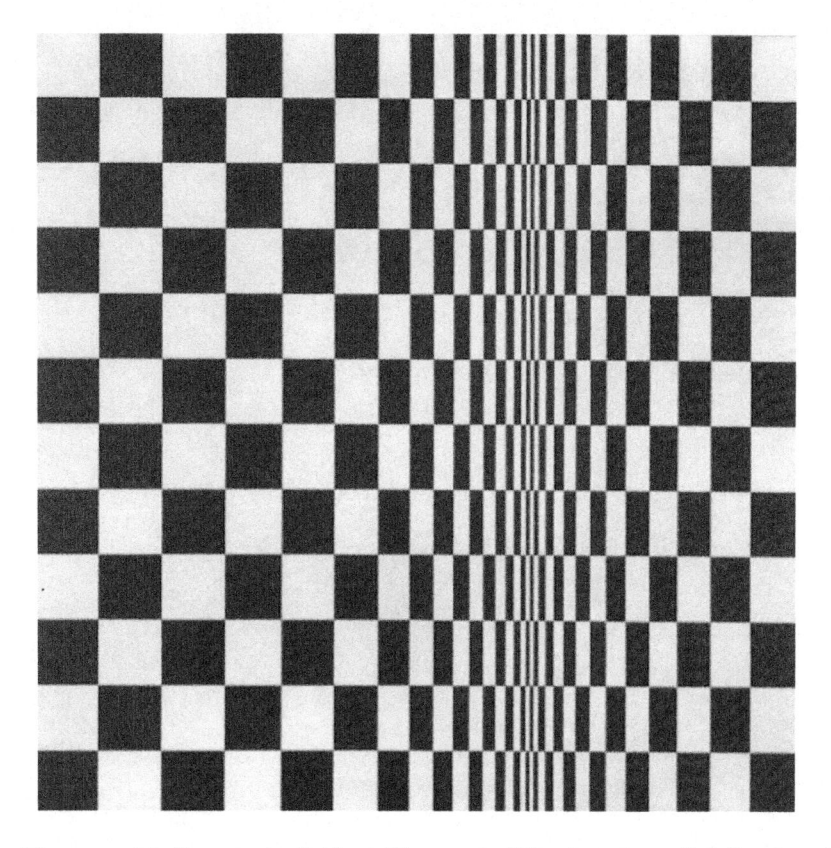

Movement in Squares by Bridget Riley part of The Arts Council Collection

to trial different hypotheses about what is being viewed but, at the time, it was both novel and stunning.

Movement in Squares?

Black... white... black... white... black... white...,
black/white, black/white, black/white,
black... white... black... white... black... white.
Squeezed in, pulled out, my poor head churns.

White always goes first you declare.
It's not as if black wasn't there
first... last..., first/last, first... last...
In group or out, prejudice burns.

Yes, we don't want to disappoint,
Maybe we've reached a tipping point?
On... off..., on/off, on... off...
Squeezed in, pulled out, how my heart yearns

for a world where we celebrate
colour and everyone's fate,
good... bad..., good/bad, good...bad...
is well deserved, in just returns.

Dialogue

You did what?

I shot him.

Why on Earth?

I didn't mean to, it was an accident. But he shouldn't have come at me in the dark like that.

Is he okay? No, scrub that, after his behaviour yesterday I don't really care. What actually happened?

Well, you know the path at the back of the Tennis Center?

The one right by the reservoir?

No, the other one, between the two. Well, I was out jogging, or at least trying to and he jumped out at me. From a bush beside the path.

You're joking!

No, stupid fucker thought he'd scare me for a laugh. Must have spotted me earlier and nipped across the grass to get round in front.

Arrogant sod. I guess his plan worked.

Yup, I jumped through the roof but fortunately that self-defence training we did kicked in, remember that fundamental pistol course with the cute instructor? I drew on him.

What, you were carrying while jogging? As for fortunately, I'm not so sure, I don't think you're going to live this one down easily. Anyway, why were you armed?

It was only a small calibre pistol. I don't always feel safe in Central Park.

Nor do I but I don't carry a gun when running, just this.

Oh yeah, a rape alarm always works, right? Much better to be prepared for anything, I've got pepper spray as well as the gun.

Remind me not to bump into you on a dark night. So how did you end up shooting him?

Simples, he didn't stop when I shouted, 'Freeze or I'll shoot', assumed I'd recognise him. Some joke, eh?

Certainly backfired on him. How badly is he hurt?

Not very, I didn't aim to kill, and the bullet clipped his shoulder. The emergency room medics fixed him up easily. He's a bit pissed at me though.

I'm not surprised, you can't go around shooting the boss without expecting some comeback.

Well, he should bloody well start behaving like a boss then.

Setting Fire

In the grim light of early dawn Ray took a deep breath. He carefully lit the fire lighter, waited a moment for the flame to build then rolled it under the caravan. This was the key moment. *Had he used enough kindling? Would it catch light?* "Yesss." he sighed happily, letting out the breath that he hadn't realised that he was still holding as the flickering flame built quickly into a small fire. Things were looking good; he should go now, before anyone noticed his presence. Hugging his rucksack tightly to stop the empty cans of lighter fluid clattering, he jogged up the coastal path to a nearby spot that overlooked the holiday park.

Ray was in luck, he had just found a dry cliff edge to lean against when the caravan itself caught light. The small fire he had started grew rapidly into a huge, multi-coloured conflagration as the different plastics burned. As he watched the blaze Ray couldn't stop grinning, he felt great, invincible even. He didn't believe that there was another feeling that could begin to touch this rapture, he was part of the fire itself, dancing and writhing alongside the flames. This blissful reverie was shattered when the caravan's gas bottles exploded with a deafening, double retort that echoed across the cliffs leaving Ray gasping with delight. He would be late for work that morning but no matter.

At the same time as Ray finally turned up for his shift DI Trevor Mawgan, flat white in one hand and a sugary doughnut in the other, elbowed the station door open. The duty constable didn't look up from his newspaper but mouthed, "Incident room, twenty minutes, there's been another one. Caravan at the holiday park, Trumpton are still there and the Super's out for your guts."

Trevor groaned, every time he'd planned on a quiet day catching up on paperwork, something like this happened. Come to think of it, there'd been way too many fires of late. At this rate he would have retired before he'd got his case notes sorted and filed. *How many weeks to go was it now, seven or eight maybe?"* "And counting." He'd spoken aloud.

The constable looked up "What?"

"Nothing, nothing, just wondering how many caravan fires it was now."

"This morning's the twelfth, seems like the perp's graduated from derelict tourers left by farm workers and is now starting on the mobile home parks."

"Not sure how I feel about that, those places are ruddy eyesores. Completely spoil the look of the coastline and fill up every sodding school holiday with light fingered chavs and drunken tarts."

"Tut, tut, now sir, we can't all have what we want."

The two shared a rueful grin and Trevor made his way to his office upstairs where managed to eat at least half the doughnut before his DS, Annie Pinkman, found him.

"Meeting's starting boss, by the way the arson investigation was upgraded earlier this morning and we've been assigned two uniform. I've had them set up an incident room."

Trevor's eyebrows shot up at the news. Somebody important must have got at the Super, the perp had getting his rocks off making old caravans into bonfires for months now and today was the first he'd heard of any realistic action being taken. *Maybe one of the mobile homes belonged to a nob?*

It turned out that Trevor's guess wasn't so very far off, the Lord Lieutenant himself had had his nose put out of joint by this morning's caravan fire. The oily black smoke from the holiday park had spread over his grouse moor and wrecked his guests' morning shooting. The Super had clearly been given an earful and, returning the favour, now gave him and Annie a bollocking for their lack of action.

Trevor swallowed, trying to keep his temper. "Sir, we've had no resources, well not until today that is and all these sites, they're so remote, no cameras no real evidence as such."

One of the uniforms perked his head up "What not even tyre tracks? Footprints?"

"Nothing to suggest any vehicles but yeah, prints from size 10 trainers, cheapo supermarket ones, common as muck."

Annie chipped in, "We do have one key finding, Trumpton say the fire accelerant being used is unusual, perp is soaking anything they can find in lighter fluid. It's bit weird as it's loads more expensive than petrol."

Ray had no idea that he was the hot topic for discussion at the police station this morning. Still wired from his exhilarating morning he was currently juggling cans of soup as he stacked the shelves in the big Tesco Extra outside town. He'd worked there three days a week for over three years now with little or no time off and had, by and large, convinced the management that he was a steady worker. His supervisor, Katie smiled indulgently at him as she rushed by to sort out the rest of the delivery.

The rest of his day was uneventful but tiring and Ray slept like a log that night. And the next. Indeed, it wasn't until the end of the week that the compulsion to burn reasserted itself. Friday night found him yet again gazing in ecstasy as flames leaped skyward. As Ray watched he wondered if, maybe he should be stricter with himself, like maybe wait a bit longer between fires.

"Nah" he shook his head as he spoke out loud, "Why bother? Holiday park's full of effing empty mobile homes, there's even another one on the other side of the bay if things were to get difficult here."

That said, he didn't see how they might, as long as he stuck to burning the old caravans, no-one seemed too bothered.

Yet Ray was wrong about that, Annie, hauled into work on a Saturday morning, had lost her temper. Having planned around a lazy morning in bed with her boyfriend followed by a bit of retail therapy she was not best pleased to find herself chasing her tail in an apparently stalled investigation.

"Has no-one got a sodding clue?" she asked the hastily assembled team.

Trevor shrugged, "Nothing new from last night, same MO, same accelerant." He wasn't sure he cared that much but he knew he ought to play ball, well at least for the next two months. He sighed.

Annie interrupted, "But sooner or later someone's going to get killed."

"Well, let's hope it's the perp." one of the uniforms sniggered but Annie was thinking.

"Shut up a moment, what if… what if we stop faffing about looking for the arsonist and try to trace that lighter fluid they're using instead? Can we do that?"

"Don't see as why not, perp's most likely local and there aren't that many places that sell lighter fluid. He or she must be getting through quarts of the bloody stuff." Trevor allowed. The two constables became animated at the thought.

"There's the DIY shops."

"You can get it at the garage, you know in the cupboard behind the cashier with all the fags etc."

"And Wilkos."

"Right, sounds like a plan, you all know what to do, divvy up the stores and report back." Trevor left the team to it, with luck, he would be back home in time for the rugby.

Now the Pirates had, against all odds, made it into the Premiership he had a duty to keep an eye on the local team, did he not?

Later that afternoon he took a call from Annie. The three of them had legged it all over town and had been unable to find any unusual sales of lighter fluid. Trevor wasn't surprised, you could buy anything on the Internet these days, but it had been a good call by Annie, and he didn't want to dampen her enthusiasm.

"We'll review the evidence from scratch on Monday, we've forensics from all the recent fires, there must be something we've missed." Trevor, distracted by noise from the telly as Bath scored a try swore and ended the call abruptly.

The review was unsuccessful, there were plenty of common factors, the most obvious one being that only uninhabited caravans and mobile homes were being targeted so they were confident that the perp had local knowledge. Unfortunately, nearly everyone in town wore trainers, the only thing they could say about their size 10 prints was that it was most likely they were looking for a male. Trevor spent the best part of the week thinking up tasks to keep the team away from the station and out of sight of the Super who, fretting about their lack of progress, was liable to bite their heads off.

Yet things changed later that week when the holiday park management took things into their own hands and employed a night watchman. He was a large lad, an ex-nightclub bouncer who took his job seriously, patrolling the park on the hour throughout the night. He was certainly effective, literally bumping into Ray, who had grown over-confident, on only his third shift. Ray was so startled that he had not been able to think of any reason to justify his presence and the night watchman became immediately suspicious. Seizing Ray by his rucksack, he hoisted him into the air and bellowed into his ear.

"What the fuck do you think you are doing?"

But, in his desperation, Ray wriggled violently and managed to slip out of the rucksack and onto all fours. Scrambling up he promptly sprinted for the exit and the coastal path without looking back. The night watchman gave chase but, clearly not as fit as he thought he was, had been forced to give up as Ray sped uphill, dodging the gorse bushes and vaulting rocks.

When the holiday park manager brought the rucksack into the station the next morning Annie was delighted. She pulled on a pair of blue nitrile gloves and went quickly through it before handing it over to forensics. There wasn't much, just four yellow cans of Ronsonol lighter fluid, a box of Zippo firelighters and a packet of Cook's matches. It took her less than five minutes searching online to discover that all the brands were all sold by Tesco.

The team hung their heads as Trevor, bemoaning the gods of fate that sent him incompetent officers, let rip at their stupidity. He stopped for breath and before he could launch into another diatribe Annie grabbed the nearest constable, Jem. The two of them literally scurried down to the large Tesco Extra just off the nearby ring road.

There they were surprised to be greeted promptly and ushered in to see the manager straight away. He too was surprised to see them.

"My God that was quick, we've only just called in the police."

Annie and Jem looked blank. "Called us about what, sir?"

The manager's eyebrows shot up at her ignorance, "You know, the pilfering. Head office organised an external audit and we've lost inventory in several areas. Weirdest thing is most of it is from household essentials, bulky stuff that's not usually a shoplifter's target. It must be an inside job."

"Sorry, what's household essentials?" asked Jem.

"You know, bits and pieces like er… bin liners, ironing board covers and vacuum cleaner bags. Umm… shoe polish and Tupperware. Oh and lighters and matches."

Annie had been about to interrupt, surely identifying the fire setter was more important than petty theft but, at the manager's last words, the penny dropped.

"Would that include lighter fluid, say Ronsonol, sir?" she asked.

"Yes, that's one of the most surprising things, we must have lost buckets of the stuff."

She groaned, they should have discovered this weeks ago. Well better late than never, "We're going to need a staff list with the names of everyone with access to lighter fluid.

"Well that should cut the list down quite a bit, we've got a separate flammables store." He pressed a button on his desk and, leaning into the nearby microphone called, "Duty supervisor to the manager's office please."

His voice had barely finished echoing around the store when Katie rushed in.

" Who has access to the household essentials stock?" he demanded.

"What you mean, as well as Ray?" she qualified, "He's been in charge of inflammables for over a year now." She looked at the police officers, "Funny that you should be asking about him, he didn't turn up for his shift today, Most unlike him."

Annie and Jem took Ray's ID photo and contact details back to the station, but all further searches proved fruitless. It was as if he had vanished into thin air. It took a few weeks but, with no more fires, things at the station settled down into their usual routine. The Super found himself a new stick to berate them with but Trevor, mulling over his retirement plans, didn't care.

Indeed, one day a year or so later, found Trevor sitting comfortably in the pub, reading in his paper about fires at holiday caravan sites at a resort miles away, on the North Coast of Devon. He smiled to himself, raised his glass and turned the page.

Faringdon Writers was started in 2014 by a group of people with a passion for writing.

Our members hail from a wide variety of walks of life, of different ages and with different skill levels.

Meetings take place once a month to share experiences, interests, and issues.

As critical friends we support and challenge each other to further our creativity as well as our enthusiasm. We look at and consider writing in a variety of genres and styles and discuss issues such as marketing and publishing.

Meetings consist of an initial round-up of our month's writing, followed by a talk on a specific aspect. Occasionally there are visiting speakers or a workshop to explore new ideas. There is always time to do a little bit of practical work with a cup of tea and a biscuit. If not able to meet in person, we are always happy to meet up via Zoom!

You are more than welcome to come and join us.

For more information visit our Facebook page 'Faringdon Writers' or contact us at <u>faringdonwriters@gmail.com</u>

Printed in Great Britain
by Amazon